# PETER J. CULLINANE

# Who are you really?

## a seeker's guide to faith

McCRIMMONS

# Acknowledgments

The Scripture passages in this book have been taken from several different translations, including:

*The Jerusalem Bible* (London: Darton, Longman and Todd, 1966)

*The New Jerusalem Bible* (London: Darton, Longman and Todd, 1990)

*The New American Bible* (New York: Oxford University Press, 1995)

*The Grail* (Psalms), (London: Collins, 1963)

*The New Revised Standard Version of the Bible*, Division of Christian Education of the National Council of Churches in the U.S.A., 1989.

For the sake of consistency, all verse numbers found in the Scripture citations herein refer to those used by the NRSV. Therefore, wording of passages found in this book may be different from what is found in the NRSV edition.

Quotes from the following books are used with permission:

Bassett, Bernard. *The Noonday Devil*. London: Burns and Oates, 1964.

Murray, John Courtney. *The Problem of God: Yesterday and Today*. New Haven, CT: Yale University Press, 1964.

Baxter, James K. *Song to the Holy Spirit: The Collected Poems of J.K. Baxter*. New York: Oxford University Press, 1979.

Steindl-Rast, David. *A Listening Heart*. New York: The Crossroad Publishing Company, 1999.

Twenty-Third Publications
A Division of Bayard
185 Willow Street
P.O. Box 180
Mystic, CT 06355
(860) 536-2611 or (800) 321-0411
www.twentythirdpublications.com
ISBN:1-58595-379-2

McCrimmon Publishing Co. Ltd
10/12 High Street
Great Wakering, Essex England
SS3 OEQ
01702 218956
www.mccrimmons.com
ISBN: 0 85597 664 0

# Dedication

To all who have enabled me to see

Bonito

# Contents

# PART II

# Introduction
## Facing the Questions

Who is that sitting on a small, rotating planet gliding through a large, cold universe? It's you, of course. It really is. And where do you think you are going? You're riding further out into space as the universe still expands. Some scientists say that when it loses its impetus it will collapse inward. By then, you will be in a grave somewhere. So let's look there for a moment.

There's someone sitting by your grave; someone who loved you a lot. By now the flesh you nourished and protected has fallen off you. But years down the road, there will be no one sitting there. In time, no one will even be thinking about you. In the long history of the universe your life seems to have been no more than a flicker. And so you might wonder: did my life really matter?

Count yourself lucky if you got a decent burial. Human history is scarred all over by the slaughter and extermination of people in every era. Many whose lives were unjustly and brutally taken from them pleaded with God to save them. But God didn't seem to hear.

Today we are more sophisticated. We have new ways of combating illness, but also new ways of killing people. Better technology and democratic processes haven't stopped bad things from happening. Yet good things are happening as well—wonderful things, beautiful things! But pause for a moment and consider these questions:

- Do you sense that the bad experiences are not how things are meant to be, and that the good experiences say something about how things are meant to be?

- Why does life seem to be like a promise that is not yet fulfilled? And why does it seem to promise what it can't deliver?

- Why do you instinctively try to make sense of your life? And can it really make sense if it doesn't include a future?

- Why is a child's smile so wonderful if one day it will be wiped out forever? When you hug a child to assure the little one that all will be well, are you just taking part in a massive, terrible deception, if in the end all might not be well?

- Why does your heart tell you that some things are meant to be forever? And how do you know if your heart is right?

- Why is it that two people can still be discovering how wonderful the other is after a lifetime together? Evidently, there's much more to who they really are than what's on their driver's license or their *curriculum vitae*.

- If there is much more to you than where you come from and what you do, what is this much more? Who are you really?

And further: is faith in God something extra that you can take or leave without it making any difference to who and what you are? Surely one can be a good person without religion. Then again, what would be the point of being good, since good people can suffer as much as bad people, and sometimes unjustly? If you want to make sense of that, what you are looking for is meaning. You don't automatically have meaning just because you are a good person. Even good persons need to know their lives have meaning.

So where do we look for meaning? Is it something you can just decide for yourself, or is it bigger than that—something that links you with others? The deepest question in every human heart is: does my life ultimately matter?

Everything else about your life hinges on the answer to that question.

So what is a human being? Is a person whatever biotechnology might one day be able to produce? And produce to somebody else's order?

You only have one shot at your life. So is it okay for your life to be determined mainly by other people's preferences—their social ambitions, their economic priorities, their political agendas? Perhaps those who have power to limit your options believe that as individuals they have a right to do whatever they choose. Where does that leave you?

Do you have a value greater than your usefulness to others? And what about those who can't be "useful" due to disability or illness or lack of opportunity? What is a person's value based on?

In these pages I will invite you to look to where others have found meaning. Where others have been can be a vantage point from which to make your own discoveries. I hope the view will give you great joy in knowing who you really are and how much your life really matters.

What I shall share with you is what I have seen and heard and know. "This text was not born at the writing desk" (Martin Buber). At times I will be talking about "we" and "us"; that's because we all face the same questions. When I refer to "you" and "your," that's because I am respecting your individuality and addressing the question: who are you—personally—really?

In this book we'll cover a range of topics, touching on things you might have thought were unrelated to each other. What they have in common is that they all have something to do with who you are and how you can know this. Each later chapter builds on the earlier chapters, so they need to be taken in sequence—the way you read a story. It's all about making connections.

At the end of each chapter, you'll find brief exercises under the heading For Practice, as well as selected passages from the psalms, Scripture, and Christian writers to use for prayer. These are important to do because they will help you make your own discoveries about what is covered in each chapter, and find answers to some of the questions you have about life, meaning, and God.

There is someone waiting for you at the end of this journey—someone you will enjoy meeting.

We shall not cease from exploration
And the end of all our exploring
Will be to arrive where we started
And know the place for the first time.

T.S. Eliot, *Little Gidding*

# For Practice

• Which of the questions found here in the Introduction held particular interest for you? Reflect for a while on what this might say about where you are in your life right now.

# Part I

# 1 Your Past

You can find out a lot about yourself from both science and religious faith. And that's good news on both fronts.

Science shows that at the time of your conception there were more than a million sperm competing to fertilize a waiting ovum. One did so. Every other combination of sperm and ovum would have been a different person from you. The one moment in the whole history of the universe when any of them could have come into existence passed at that moment. They will never exist. At the one moment when you could have come into existence, you did.

*At the one moment when you could have come into existence, you did.*

Science also shows that from conception you were a new being—not just a part of your mother or father. Genetically, you were already your own self. There was no other threshold you had to cross over to become the person you are now. It was already you. All you needed was nurture and time to develop.

The moment you came into existence depended on the dynamics of love and body chemistry and circumstances and your parents' personal histories, reaching back to before they met each other—and even back to before our planet was formed from the gases and dust that swirled about in space billions of years ago. You've got quite a pre-history.

Religious faith can add to what science tells you. Faith and science are two different doorways into reality. They are not even in competition with each other. Science seeks to understand everything the universe contains, including what is still waiting to be discovered. Faith is concerned with why there is a universe at all, instead of nothing. Science and faith look at the same reality—it's just that there are two, equally valid, ways of seeing it.

## For Practice

• Look at a book or video that features the early history of the universe, or the planets, and ponder your pre-history. Also ponder your destiny: you live on a planet that is about halfway through its habitable life because the sun is about halfway through its fuel supply and its own life! (See *The Planets*, BBC, 1990.) If the scientists are right, the future of the planets is not very bright. So any ultimate, worthwhile hope isn't going to come from the cosmos.

• On a clear night, away from city lights, look up at the stars and allow yourself to experience wonder.

## For Prayer

O Lord, our Lord
   how awesome is your name
      through all the earth!
You have set your majesty above the heavens!

When I see your heavens, the work of your hands,
   the moon and stars that you set in place—
What are humans that you are mindful of them,
   mere mortals that you care for them?

You have made them little less than a god,
   crowned them with glory and honor.
Yet you have given them rule
   over the works of your hands,
   put all things at their feet:
All sheep and oxen,
   even the beasts of the field,
The birds of the air, the fish of the sea,
   and whatever swims the paths of the seas.
O Lord, our Lord,
   how awesome is your name
   through all the earth!

*Psalm 8:1, 3–9*

IT TOOK THE UNIVERSE A VERY LONG TIME to be ready for us. The galaxies themselves had to be formed (about 15 billion years ago), including eventually, our own sun and solar system (about 5 billion years ago). Then it took another billion years before the earliest forms of life appeared, and another long time before mammals emerged (about 67 million years ago), and another long time before humans appeared (less than 2 million years ago.) The whole process began about 20 billion years ago, and so humans are late arrivals. If the time-scale were compressed into a 24-hour period, humans arrived only a couple of minutes ago.

But we are not aliens. Human life is part of the universe itself. Activities that are distinctively human, such as love and smiles, laughter, music, and song, are all made from the fibers of the planet. In a real sense, the planet itself finds expression in us. It finds its voice in our voices.

# 2 Two Ways of Seeing

When you look out on the world at the beginning of each new day, there are two ways of seeing it. One of these ways can lead to great satisfaction; the other to sheer wonder.

First, you can see the world as our habitat where we naturally try to make ourselves comfortable. Through the sciences we explore its physical laws; through technology we harness its energies and use its resources. Within proper limits this is surely how it is meant to be. We even feel a responsibility to improve our lives in these ways, and a responsibility to use the world's resources in a sustainable way. Through work and technology and artistic creativity we develop the world, and we develop ourselves as well.

But there is another way of looking at the world, in addition to seeing it as something to be used. That is to see it as something we didn't put there in the first place. It was given to us, and behind everything "given" there is a Giver. This is what the world itself began to know from the time it attained conscious, human life. It is a characteristic of human life to recognize the world as "given" and to acknowledge a Giver.

> Because creation was entrusted to human stewardship, the natural world is not just a resource to be exploited, but also a reality to be respected and even reverenced as a gift and trust from God. (Pope John Paul II, *To the Church in Oceania*)

*We never have a right to what is pure gift. And a person can only ever be a gift—not owed nor owned.*

What is startling is that God didn't need to create the world because a God in need would not be God. So it was a choice God didn't have to make. The world's existence is, therefore, pure gift. Just try to imagine that it had been owed to you! If it wasn't, then it was gifted to you. That already says something about you.

We begin to know how much we matter when we know that God didn't need to create anything, yet wanted to. God could have chosen to create a world that didn't include you, yet God chose to create a world that would include you. Have you ever wondered why?

You were called into existence—and cared about from the beginning:

O Lord, you search me and you know me,
 you know my resting and my rising,
 you discern my purpose from afar,
You mark when I walk or lie down,
 all my ways lie open to you.
Before ever a word is on my tongue
 you know it, O Lord,
 through and through.
Behind and before you besiege me,
 your hand ever laid upon me.
Too wonderful for me, this knowledge,
 too high, beyond my reach.

It was you who created my being,
 knit me together in my mother's womb.

I thank you for the wonder of my being,
 for the wonders of all your creation.

Already you knew my soul,
my body held no secret from you
when I was being fashioned in secret
and molded in the depths of the earth.

O search me, God, and know my heart.
O test me and know my thoughts.
See that I follow not the wrong path
and lead me in the path of life eternal.

*Psalm 139:1–6, 13–15, 23–24*

The experience of wonder often accompanies the birth of a child. We seem to know intuitively that there is more to a child than can be accounted for by its parents' part in bringing it into the world.

The underlying reason for wonder remains throughout each person's life. Each one of us exists because of a choice God made: this is our great dignity, and nothing can change that. It is the basis for a whole different way of seeing yourself and every other person.

# For Practice

• Keep in mind that every person you will meet today (or have met today) was personally called into existence by God, and is a gift.

• Look into the eyes of a baby or a child and give thanks. Know that in your life, someone else has given thanks for you as well.

• Notice how often the argument in support of becoming parents through surrogacy starts from the assumption that individuals "have a right to have a child." Do they really?

# For Prayer

The heavens declare the glory of God;
the sky proclaims its builder's craft.
One day to the next takes up the story;
one night to the next
makes known the message.
There is no word, or sound;
no voice is heard;
yet their report goes forth
through all the earth.

*Psalm 19:1–4*

THE ROLE OF APPLIED SCIENCE IN ASSISTING THE PROCESSES OF CONCEPTION and birth is to be welcomed provided the methods used accord with human dignity and the meaning of marriage. Not everything that is technically possible is morally right. Newly conceived persons are meant to be the fruit of married love, not the products of laboratory processes and manufacture.

Even good and generous people can hugely underestimate the dignity of persons; for example, when they speak as if there could be "a right to have a child." We never have a right to what is pure gift. And a person can only ever be a gift—not owed nor owned. Persons are not property. Nor may little ones in the womb be used as raw material for developing vaccines, or be discarded because they don't measure up to someone else's preferences.

The potential clash between what is technically feasible and what is morally right becomes dramatic when it impinges on human nature itself. So much depends on whether we see our world and other people only as resources, or also as gifts from the hand of a divine Giver.

# 3 Coming Alive

When you begin to see your life and everything else around you as a gift, you come alive to how things really are. You begin to live in the real world.

What you see and recognize as a gift you then receive in the way that a gift is received. Your life becomes a kind of thanksgiving. The opposite of this is to take everything for granted, as if it were not a gift; as if there were no one to thank. This isn't living according to how things really are.

There is a wonderful paradox here: if neither your own existence nor the world's is owed to you, then your "poverty" is what makes you so rich—*everything* is a gift. You are surrounded by a sea of gifted existence.

Even the smallest details of creation speak to you about God, and there is enough in the smallest garden or backyard to give you reason for constant wonder. Those who are most likely not to have that experience—not to see the world as it actually is—are those in the biggest hurry and the most mobile. Those who have been slowed down or curtailed by some disability sometimes have the best view.

Noticing means standing in awe of each creature, all of whose very existence points to God.

> God is in creation as the voice is in the song.
>
> Look at the dance and you will see the Dancer.
> Anthony de Mello, SJ

Noticing also means letting yourself be caught up in beauty. The beauty we find in nature, the beauty we create in music, song, and dance, and the beauty that belongs to love, family, loyalty, and faithfulness all seem to say to us: "this is not for nothing; this is only a glimpse of something more to come."

It is not an exaggeration to say that through every detail of creation God "speaks" to us:

> The Bible conceives of everything as created by God's word, and so as actually being a word. In this world view every thing, every person, every situation is at its core a spelling out of God's faithfulness calling for a response of faith on the hearer's part. ["Let your every creature serve you: for you spoke, and they were made, you sent forth your spirit, and they were created; no one can resist your word" (Judith 16:14).]

Do not deny too quickly that you know what is meant by the poetic image, "God speaks." Yet, don't take my word for it either. Search your own awareness. We are talking about something that is easily missed, "a small, still voice," easily drowned out by our own noises, something shy that wants to be befriended.

> Only when we become ever so quiet inside do we sense in the smallest speck of reality a great Presence, both strange and familiar, waiting to meet us. Strange this Presence seems to us, because it differs from all else we know; at the

*When you begin to see your life and everything else around you as a gift, you come alive to how things really are. You begin to live in the real world.*

same time, we seem to know it more intimately than anything else we ever knew. We dread its strangeness; we long for its intimacy. It is this Presence that looks at us, when we dare to expose ourselves "on the heart's mountains," and demands our transformation: "you must change." (David Steindl-Rast, *A Listening Heart*)

# For Practice

• Take time to look at a flower or a tree, and keep on looking. If it could speak, what might it want to say to you?

• Next time you experience peace or beauty or love or belonging, notice how the experience feeds a deep longing, but never fully meets your need. What does this say to you about humankind's longing for God?

# For Prayer

Where can I go from your spirit,
   or where can I flee from your face?
If I climb the heavens, you are there.
If I lie in the grave, you are there.
If I take the wings of the dawn
   and dwell at the sea's furthest end,
   even there your hand would lead me,
   your right hand would hold me fast.
If I say: "Let the darkness hide me
   and the light around me be night,"
   even darkness is not dark for you
   and the night is as clear as the day....
                    *Psalm 139:7–12*

# 4 Looking But Not Seeing

If sometimes you find it hard to see the world as a gift, you are not alone. It seems easier just to see it as a resource—which it is. But to see it only as a resource, and to see no further than what human reason and the methods of science can see and measure, is a diminished way of seeing—which means a diminished way of living.

Such a narrow vision has an interesting history. Before the modern sciences were developed, people's ways of thinking were largely determined by culture, tradition, and the authority of those who were guardians of the tradition. But culture and tradition were often accepted uncritically, and authority was sometimes misused. There was little defense against cruelty, degradation, superstition, and fear.

Eventually the age of science dawned. The period known as the Enlightenment (from the 1600s on) gave rise to great expectations. It was thought that reason would eventually be able to explain everything there was to know. Mere tradition, and the authority of those who knew the tradition, would become irrelevant. God would be explained away as a kind of symbol we needed for making sense of our existence before we had the sciences.

Jewish and Christian faith helped to bring about this development. By teaching that the world was not inhabited by gods (pantheism), Jewish and Christian faith promoted the right of human reason to explain all aspects of the world. There was nothing to fear from reason because

> "Science without religion is lame, and religion without science is blind."
> —Albert Einstein

faith had its own different role. Even today, indigenous peoples still combine deep religious faith with their acceptance of the sciences. But Western culture and education became pervaded by the assumption that science would replace faith.

Some influential thinkers even claimed that people needed to be rid of God because it seemed that religion inhibited human self-esteem, human freedom, and human progress. Pantheistic religions, and also some misguided interpretations of Christian faith, have sometimes demeaned human dignity and hindered human progress. So it was suggested that the world would be a better place when reason completely displaced faith. But it seems not to have turned out as these thinkers expected.

> Western cultural models are enticing and alluring because of their remarkable scientific and technical cast, but regrettably there is growing evidence of their deepening human, spiritual, and moral impoverishment. (From an address by John Paul II, 1 January 2001)

Increasingly, people are becoming dissatisfied with a purely secular and materialistic interpretation of life. It doesn't satisfy the deepest yearnings of human nature. They have "had the experience but missed the meaning" (T.S. Eliot). Today, scientists are more likely to say, with Albert Einstein, that "science without religion is lame, and religion without science is blind."

Science needs religion to humanize its goals and offer ethical guidance as it advances into new arenas. Religion needs science to prevent it from receding into superstition and to infuse it with new metaphors for talking about God and God's creation. (M.M. Winstanley, "Building Bridges," in the *Journal of Youth and Theology*)

Faith and science are not dealing with different "worlds." They are two different ways of looking at the same world. They are both servants of reality. And they are both servants of the mystery of life, which is always bigger than mere answers, whether scientific or religious.

# For Prayer

As the deer longs for streams of water,
    so my soul longs for you, O God.
My being thirsts for God, the living God.
When can I go and see the face of God?
My tears have become my food day and night.
    as they daily ask,
"Where is your God?"

Why are you downcast, my soul;
    why do you groan within me?
Wait for God, whom I shall praise again,
    my savior and my God.

*Psalm 42:1–4, 5*

BECAUSE FAITH AND REASON HAVE DIFFERENT ROLES, they don't actually clash. But some of the language we use to express faith does clash with a scientific perspective. Religious language sometimes draws on images and symbols that don't depend on the findings of modern science. For example, we speak as if God is "up there," and as if God sometimes intervenes in the world from outside of it. This gives rise to the question of why God seems to intervene sometimes and not at other times. From this perspective, mysteries appear only to be problems we don't know the answers to—yet.

Some people try to get around this by bringing faith under the umbrella of human understanding. In effect, they exclude faith by excluding the existence of anything that cannot ultimately be understood by human reason. They propose "Godness in everyday life" as a substitute for a God "out there."

But faith sees God as the Source of all created existence. This makes God even closer to us than we are to ourselves. And so our ordinary existence points beyond itself to the extraordinary fact that we exist at all! This is the mystery, and always will be, because it comes from a choice God did not have to make. It is the mystery of extraordinary love, and the source of our "Godness in everyday life."

# 5 Choosing to See

You've got a choice in all this. To see the world as a "gift" and God as the giver, or not to see the world this way, is ultimately a *choice* each of us has to make because it involves going beyond the evidence. We can't see God in the way we see the world. Equally, we can't see there is no God! Whichever conclusion we come to is a position we choose on the basis of incomplete vision. Either way, we are looking at the same evidence; our choice will make the difference.

The choice we make depends on how willing we are to live with the consequences of that choice. Even in the ordinary questions we ask about life, there is always a little bit of our self invested in the question and at stake in the answer. When the question is about God, our whole existence is involved. The conclusion we reach depends on whether we are willing or not willing to live with the consequences of what we choose to believe.

> *"Knowing" God is an ongoing process of personal conversion—from seeing the world only as a resource, to seeing it also as a gift....*

In this sense, "knowing" God is an ongoing process of personal conversion—from seeing the world only as a resource, to seeing it also as a gift; from fearing the consequences of the choice we make to embracing the consequences.

The division between "seeing" and "not seeing" is not "out there" in other people; the ongoing conversion needs to take place in our own hearts. And like all conversion, this "seeing" is also a gift or grace, to be asked for and to give thanks for.

The book of Wisdom (dating from about 100 years before Christ) tried to account for how people could not "see" God. For a moment the author tried to excuse them: perhaps the very beauty of created things had led them to mistake these things for gods. But then he realized that even this could not really excuse them:

> All were foolish who were unaware of God, and who, from good things seen, have not been able to discover Him-who-is, or, by studying the works, have not recognized the Artisan. Fire, however, or wind, or the swift air, the sphere of the stars, or the mighty water or heaven's lamps, are what they have held to be the gods who govern the world.
>
> If, charmed by their beauty, they have taken these for gods, let them know how far more excellent is the Lord of these; for the original source of beauty fashioned them. And if they have been impressed by their power and energy, let them deduce from these how much mightier is he who made them, since through the grandeur and beauty of created things we may, by analogy, contemplate their Author.
>
> Yet, for these the blame is less, for perhaps they go astray only in their search for God and their eagerness to find him; familiar with his works, they investigate them and fall victim to appearances, seeing so much beauty. But even so, they have no excuse: if they are capable of acquiring enough knowledge to be able to investigate the world, how have they been so slow to find its Master? (Wisdom 13:1–9)

St. Augustine beautifully records his personal experience of this problem, showing that conversion is also the work of God's grace:

> Late have I loved you, O Beauty, ever ancient ever new, late have I loved you! You were within me, but I was outside, and it was there that I searched for you. In my unloveliness I plunged into the lovely things which you created. You were with me, but I was not with you. Created things kept me from you; But if they had not been in you they would not have been at all. You called, you shouted, and you broke through my deafness. You flashed, you shone, and you dispelled my blindness. You breathed your fragrance on me; I drew in breath and now I pant for you. I have tasted you, now I hunger and thirst for more. You touched me, and I burned for your peace. (*Confessions*)

# For Practice

• At the end of the day, take a few quiet minutes to look back over the day, remembering any moments when you might have felt uneasy, and any when you felt glad. Then look to see what choices or decisions led to those feelings.

# For Prayer

Have mercy on me, God, in your kindness.
In your compassion blot out my offense.
O wash me more and more from my guilt
 and cleanse me from my sin.
My offenses truly I know them;
 my sin is always before me.
Against you, you alone, have I sinned;
 what is evil in your sight I have done.
That you may be justified when you give sentence
 and be without reproach when you judge.
O see, in guilt was I born,
 a sinner was I conceived.

Indeed you love truth in the heart;
 then in the secret of my heart
 teach me wisdom.
O purify me, then I shall be clean;
O wash me, I shall be whiter than snow.
Make me hear rejoicing and gladness,
 that the bones you have crushed may revive.
From my sins turn away your face
 and blot out all my guilt.

A pure heart create for me, O god,
 put a steadfast spirit within me.
Do not cast me away from your presence,
 nor deprive me of your Holy Spirit.

For in sacrifice you take no delight,
 burnt offering from me you would refuse,
 my sacrifice, a contrite spirit.
 A humbled, contrite heart you will not spurn.
 *Psalm 51:1–11, 17*

# 6 To Dust You Shall Return (Genesis 3:19)

Nature speaks to us about the beauty and power of God. But it can't tell us what God is thinking, or what God's purpose is. Nature does provide signs of God's care:

> Throughout history even to the present day, there is found among different peoples a certain awareness of a hidden power, which lies behind the course of nature and the events of human life. At times there is present even a recognition of a supreme being....This awareness and recognition results in a way of life that is imbued with a deep religious sense. (Second Vatican Council, *On Non-Christian Religions*)

Something makes us feel we are made for life, not death. We want our life to have meaning; we yearn to make sense of it all. But nature sends us mixed signals, and it can't assure us that our yearnings for life and love and meaning are going to be fulfilled.

Something also tells us that we need to do what is right and avoid what is wrong, and that our choices matter. We have a sense of being accountable. But nature can't assure us that our wrong-doings are not going to be held against us. Some practices of natural religions suggest that their adherents are never really sure how they stand with God.

We can only know God's intentions if God chooses to reveal more than what is revealed through nature. That is why we look to where God has become involved in people's lives. The signs of God's saving power in the lives of people are the signs of what God is doing in human history. In this way, time and history are revealed as having a goal and a purpose. The meaning of our lives, and of the cosmos, too, is to be found there.

For those who tried to find meaning just from the cosmos, time was the never-ending cycle of its seasons. The myths were as close as they could get to meaning.

> A robin with no Christian name ran through
> The Robin-Anthem which was all it knew,
> And rustling flowers for some third party waited
> To say which pairs, if any, should be mated.
>
> Not one of them was capable of lying,
> There was not one which knew that it was dying
> Or could have with a rhythm or a rhyme
> Assumed responsibility for time.
>
> W.H. Auden, *Their Lonely Betters*

*We can only know God's intentions if God chooses to reveal more than what is revealed through nature.*

The revealed faith of ancient Israel was different from cosmic and natural religion. Theirs was the story of God's involvement with people "chosen" to know God's purpose. Yet, they, too, had to learn that they could not bring about the fulfillment of their own deepest yearnings:

> As a woman about to give birth writhes and cries out in pains so were we in your presence, O Lord. We conceived and writhed in pain giving birth to wind. Salvation we have not achieved for the earth, the inhabitants of the world cannot bring it forth. (Isaiah 26:17–18)

Superstition also looks, in vain, to the cosmos for the meaning of human events:

When you come into the land which the Lord, your God, is giving you, you shall not learn to imitate the abominations of the peoples there. Let there not be found among you anyone who sacrifices his son or daughter in the fire, nor a fortune-teller, soothsayer, charmer, diviner, or caster of spells, nor one who consults ghost and spirits or seeks oracles from the dead. Anyone who does such things is an abomination to the Lord....You, however, must be faithful towards the Lord, your God...The Lord, your God, will raise up a prophet like me from your own kinsmen, to him you shall listen. (Deuteronomy 18:9–13, 15)

God's involvement in their history revealed a God who was faithful to them, even though they were unfaithful and unworthy. This double experience—their own unworthiness and God's love—led them to a profound hope; a hope that seemed greater than every setback. It led them to expect someone that God would send to fulfill their yearning for life and meaning.

The people who walked in darkness have seen a great light; upon those who dwelt in the land of gloom a light has shone. You have brought them abundant joy and great rejoicing....For a child is born to us, a Son is given us; upon his shoulder dominion rests. They name him Wonder-Counselor, God-hero, Father-forever, Prince of Peace. (Isaiah 9:2–3, 6)

Jesus' coming and his faithfulness would do what we could not do for ourselves.

# For Practice

- Spend some time at a cemetery thinking about those who once lived as you do now.
- Read and reflect on Isaiah 40:1–11.

# For Prayer

To you, Lord, I cried
    to my God I made appeal:
"What profit would my death be,
    my going to the grave?
Can dust give you praise or proclaim your truth?"

The Lord listened and had pity.
The Lord came to my help.
For me you have changed
    my mourning into dancing,
    you removed my sackcloth
    and clothed me with joy.

So my soul sings psalms to you unceasingly.
O Lord, my God, I will thank you forever.
*Psalm 30:8–12*

# 7 Breakthrough

You have heard the saying "it seems too good to be true." Well, the mysteries of faith are like that: they are marvelous because they are true, and too marvelous for our understanding.

When the time came for the fulfillment of God's promises, what God did exceeded all expectations:

> In times past, God spoke in fragmentary and varied ways to our ancestors through the prophets; in this, the final age, he has spoken to us in the person of his Son, whom he has made heir of all things and through whom he first created the universe. (Hebrews 1:1–2)

Referring to their own religious practices, the Letter to the Hebrews highlights the insufficiency of all previous religion:

> Since the law is only a shadow of the good things to come…it can never make perfect those who come to worship by the same sacrifices that they offer continually each year…. In those sacrifices there is only a yearly remembrance of sins, for it is impossible that the blood of bulls and goats take sins away. For this reason, when he came into the world, he said: "Sacrifice and offering you did not desire, but a body you prepared for me; holocausts and sin offerings you took no delight in. Then I said, 'as is written of me in the scroll, Behold, I come to do your will, O God.'" (Hebrews 10:1–7)

The opening of John's gospel is majestic but simple and to the point:

> In the beginning was the Word: the Word was with God and the Word was God. He was with God in the beginning. Through him all things came to be; not one thing had its being but through him. The Word was made flesh, he lived among us, and we saw his glory, the glory that is his as the only Son of the Father, full of grace and truth. (John 1:1–3, 14)

*That God would enter human history and human life in this way is astonishing. It completely overturns our instinctive way of thinking about God.*

That God would enter human history and human life in this way is astonishing. It completely overturns our instinctive way of thinking about God. And that human beings could mean so much to God is cause for "deep wonder."

> …deep amazement at the worth and dignity of the human person is another name for the gospel…for Christianity. (Pope John Paul II, *The Redeemer of the Human Race*)

## For Practice

• A story from World War I tells that one Christmas night soldiers from both sides left their trenches to greet each other in the spirit of Christmas. It seems that God's coming among us in a lowly way—that is, as a human being born in a manger—contains huge power to change things.

• What do you think of G.K. Chesterton's remark: "it's not that Christianity has been tried and found wanting; it's that Christianity hasn't yet been tried"?

## For Prayer

You do not ask for sacrifice and offerings,
    but an open ear.
You do not ask for holocaust and victim.
Instead, here am I.

In the scroll of the book it stands written
    that I should do your will.
My God, I delight in your law
    in the depth of my heart.

*Psalm 40:6–8*

THE STORY OF JESUS' CONCEPTION highlights the gift of our salvation; it was not something we could achieve for ourselves. It is God who makes the breakthrough.

In the sixth month the angel Gabriel was sent by God to a town in Galilee called Nazareth, to a virgin betrothed to a man named Joseph, of the House of David; and the virgin's name was Mary. He went in and said to her, "Rejoice, you who enjoy God's favor! The Lord is with you." She was deeply disturbed by these words and asked herself what this greeting could mean. But the angel said to her, "Mary, do not be afraid; you have won God's favor. Look! You are to conceive in your womb and bear a son, and you must name him Jesus. He will be great and will be called Son of the Most High. The Lord God will give him the throne of his ancestor David; he will rule over the House of Jacob for ever and his reign will have no end." Mary said to the angel, "But how can this come about, since I have no knowledge of man?" The angel answered, "The Holy Spirit will come upon you, and the power of the Most High will cover you with its shadow. And so the child will be holy and will be called Son of God. And I tell you this too: your cousin Elizabeth also, in her old age, has conceived a son, and she whom people called barren is now in her sixth month, for nothing is impossible to God." Mary said, "I am the servant of the Lord, let it happen to me as you have said." And the angel left her. (Luke 1:26–38)

# 8 Injustice, Suffering, and Death

How much you matter to God is revealed even more through the mysteries of sin and suffering. What we might have thought was a case against God reveals a more wonderful God.

So how did evil and suffering get into God's creation at all? How could a God who is loving and powerful allow terrible things to happen? The question is not so much about "how," but about "why." It is a question of meaning.

The entry of sin into history is pictured in an early biblical story. Adam and Eve, who represent all of us and the kind of things we do, are seen in the Garden of Eden. This symbolizes what it is like to receive the gift of life with wonder, thanksgiving, joy, and simple trust.

But instead of receiving their existence as a gift, they wanted to claim it as a right. They wanted to be on equal footing with God. But what isn't owed to us can only be a gift. So their desire to take ownership of it and be independent of God was a distortion of themselves. "Punishment" is not God's doing:

> Do not court death by your erring way of life, nor draw to yourselves destruction by the works of your hands. Because God did not make death, nor does God rejoice in the destruction of the living. (Wisdom 1:12–13)

That we would want to bring such harm on ourselves is a mystery. Adam and Eve are depicted as having been put up to it by the one Scripture calls "the father of lies," the deceiver, the seducer, the one who wants our death.

To overturn this travesty and restore us to a relationship of trust in God, One who was "with God from the beginning and was God" did not cling to his divine status and became as we are, even to the point of experiencing death, and an unjust death at that. By choosing to be faithful to his mission even when it was going to cost him his life, Jesus showed us that God really can be trusted, even when evil and injustice are doing their best. Total, loving trust allows God full sway over one's life. And when God's power in us is so complete, it shows up as resurrection.

One of Christianity's earliest hymns has been recorded for us by Paul in his letter to the Christians at Philippi:

> Though he was in the form of God,
> He did not deem equality with God
>     something to be grasped at.
> Rather, he emptied himself
>     and took the form of a slave,
>     being born in the likeness of men.
> He became as we humans are;
> And being as we are,
>     he was humbler yet,
>     even to accepting death,
>     death on a cross.
> Because of this,
> God highly exalted him
>     and bestowed on him the name
>     above every other name,
>     so that at Jesus' name
>     every knee must bend
>     in the heavens, on the earth,
>     and under the earth,
> and every tongue proclaim
>     to the glory of God the Father:
> Jesus Christ is Lord!
>
> *Philippians 2:6–11*

The Jews of Paul's time found this message a "scandal" and the Greeks called it madness. But for Christians, what God had done was reason for great joy. Now they knew that no matter how bad a situation might be:

> neither death nor life, no angel, no prince, nothing that exists, nothing still to come, not any power, or height or depth, nor any created thing, can ever come between us and the love of God, made visible in Christ Jesus our Lord. (Romans 8:38–39)

Trusting that his Father would not fail him, Jesus allowed injustice and death to take him. Their victory was short, however; they had become instrumental in their own defeat.

Knowing Christ's victory enables Christians to look the full, terrible reality of human suffering and cruelty in the eye. Patience in the presence of evil or suffering when there is nothing more we can do about it is more than just a virtue. It witnesses to what Christians already know about the wonderful outcome of all history. They can face whatever comes. They have the peace of Christ, a peace the world cannot give.

Not all suffering is related to sin. But what God has revealed through Christ's death and resurrection is a purpose so great that suffering and evil, even at their worst, cannot defeat it. This does not answer all our questions or take away our pain, but it points to an answer more marvelous than any we could have expected. Knowing that God can be trusted absolutely is what counts. We can live with unresolved questions when we know that.

It also gives us our greatest incentive for giving life our best. Why would we, if we didn't know it was all worthwhile? Even a relatively untroubled life can become tedious if we can't see meaning in it. Conversely, there isn't much people can't live through if they know there is meaning.

Far from despairing in the presence of evil, we can respond with compassion and creativity.

*What God has revealed through Christ's death and resurrection is a purpose so great that suffering and evil, even at their worst, cannot defeat it.*

Compassion and forgiveness are among the higher achievements of the human spirit. But they are possible only because there is sin and suffering, and because we know that sin and suffering don't have the last word.

As children we learned that God was good and loving. It was true, but it was more true than we knew. It seems that a world in which God comes close to us in our sins and suffering is somehow a greater creation than one in which there would have been no need for compassion and forgiveness.

Suffering and sorrow can be transformed through the way we receive and use them:

> In the saving program of Christ…suffering is in the world in order to release love, in order to give birth to works of love towards others, and in order to transform the whole of human civilization into a "civilization of love."…In (this) persons discover themselves, their own humanity, their own dignity, their own mission. (Pope John Paul II, *On the Christian Meaning of Suffering*)

# For Practice

• Christ's victory over evil continues to be revealed in the experience of people who, like him, trust God absolutely when they are the victims of injustice and tragedy. Despite itself, evil now serves the cause of Christ's gospel. Reflect, for example, on the following excerpts from the last letters of people who were awaiting execution, after they had opposed Hitler and been found out:

*Marie Kuderikova was born on March 24, 1921, worked in a factory after leaving secondary school; was active in an illegal organization, betrayed in December 1941, arrested, and executed in Breslau on March 26, 1943. Here is what she wrote to her parents on that day:*

My dear parents, my beloved little mother and father, my only sister, and my little brother…Today, the 26th March, 1943, at half past six in the evening, two days having reached my 22nd birthday, I shall draw my last breath. And yet, up to the last moment, to live and to hope. I have always had the courage to live. Moreover, I am not losing it in the face of what is called death. I should like to take upon myself all your sorrow and all your pain. I feel in myself the strength to bear it for you too, and the desire to take it with me.…

Today is a beautiful day. You are somewhere in the fields or in the little garden. Do you feel as I do that fragrance, that loveliness? It is as though I had an intimation of it today. I was out walking, I was in the open air, which was full of the essence of Spring, of warmth, the shimmer and scent of memories. The naked nerve of the soul was stirred by the poetry of the commonplace, the smell of boiled potatoes, smoke and the clatter of spoons, birds, sky, being alive—the everyday pulse beat of life. Love it, love one another, learn love, defend love, spread love.…

I feel so much warmth and love, so much faith, so much resolution, that I spread out my arms and stretch out my hands, that you may feel it too, that you may receive it. I am not afraid of what is coming. Always, even when I have failed and hurt others, I have felt an urge to the good, the sublime, the human. My whole life has been beautiful.…

Beloved people, dear life, and dear world, I kneel before you, you most precious beings in my life, and ask for love and forgiveness. I ask forgiveness for everything and of everyone who I might have ever injured.…I kiss your hands and thank you with all my heart, with all my soul, in this the most solemn hour of my life.

Your loving daughter,
Marie Kuderikova

*Peter Habernoll was born in 1924, was recruited for military service at the age of seventeen. Arrested on March 27, 1944, having been denounced by a comrade, he was condemned to death on July 14, 1944,* and executed by firing squad on September 20, 1944.

You dear ones—my dear little mum. The hour has struck, and I am calm as I have never before been in my life, and full of confidence.…The Lord is close to me and has stretched out his hands to me, and he has given me strength. He will not withhold it from you.…

*This is from a letter to Peter's mother after his death:*

Dear Frau Karen Habernoll: Your son Peter wanted me to write something about his last moments. He died fully composed, brave and calm.…He went to eternity about 4:50 o'clock. The verdict was read to him at 4:30. A few seconds before his death I said farewell to him and told him quietly to pray. In reply he said to me, "God is with me." Looking towards heaven, erect and composed, he collapsed. It was as if the breath of God were about him. His wish was that you should not mourn. May he find in God the fulfillment of his young life. And may God take him up into his eternal dwelling.

Yours sincerely,
G. Jurytko, Catholic Chaplain

*Kim Malthe-Bruun, born on July 8, 1923, in Canada, was a resident in Copenhagen and active in transporting arms. The death sentence was carried out by firing squad. This is from a letter of farewell to his sweetheart:*

Western Prison, German Prison, Cell 411
April 4, 1945

My own little sweetheart: today I was put on trial and condemned to death. What terrible news for a little girl only 20 years old!… And what shall I write now? What notes are to go into this, my swan-song? The time is short, and there are so many thoughts. What is the final and most precious gift that I can make to you? What do I possess that I can give you in farewell, in order that you may live on, grow and become an adult, in sorrow and yet with a happy smile?

We sailed upon the wild sea, we met each other in the trustful way of playing children, and we loved each other. We still love each other and we shall continue to do so. But one day a storm tore us asunder; I struck a reef and went down but you were washed up on another shore, and you will live on in a new world....

You will live on and meet other marvelous adventures. But promise me one thing—you owe this to me because of everything for which I have lived—promise me that the thought of me will never stand between you and life....

*And this excerpt is from a farewell letter to his mother:*

Dear Mother: Today, together with Jörgen, Nils, and Ludwig, I was arraigned before a military tribunal. We were condemned to death. I know that you are a courageous woman, and that you will bear this....I have traveled a road that I have never regretted. I have never evaded the dictate of my heart, and now things seem to fall into place. I am not old, I should not be dying, yet it seems so natural to me, so simple....The time is short, I cannot properly explain it, but my soul is perfectly at rest....Jörgen is sitting here before me writing to his two-year-old daughter, a letter for the day of her Confirmation.... Finally, there is a girl whom I call mine. Make her realize that the stars still shine and that I have been only a milestone on her road. Help her on: she can still become very happy.

In haste, your eldest child and only son, Kim

(These letters come from the book *Dying We Live: The Final Messages and Records of the Resistance*, Helmut Gollwitzer, ed; Harper Collins, 1983.)

# For Prayer

My spirit is faint within me;
  my heart is dismayed.
I remember the days of old;
I ponder all your deeds;
  the works of your hands, I recall.
I stretch out my hands to you:
I thirst for you like a parched land.

Hasten to answer me, Lord;
  for my spirit fails me.
Do not hide your face from me,
  lest I become like those descending to the pit.
At dawn let me hear of your kindness,
  for in you I trust.

*Psalm 143:4–8*

# 9 Jesus of Nazareth

One day two of John the Baptist's disciples followed Jesus along the riverbank. When they asked where he was living, he invited them to "Come and see." What that meeting did to them was fondly recalled by the apostle John many years later. He even records the time of day. After all, it was the most decisive moment of John's life. He gave the rest of his life over to being a follower of Jesus (see John 1:35–42).

Many of those who met Jesus of Nazareth found themselves wanting to be with him for long periods at a time. What they experienced in his company was above all a deep reassurance. Even before they knew who he really was (which they came to realize after his resurrection), what they seemed to know when they were with him was that they mattered to God. And when you matter to God, you matter! You matter regardless of anything and everything that could ever happen to you. Knowing this changes everything. It is life-giving, even in the face of death.

Jesus' followers were shattered when they saw him put to death. But then the joy of seeing him alive three days later gave them even greater reason for hope than they had before his death. Now they knew that no evil of any kind, sin, injustice, or death itself, could stand in the way of what God was doing in our history. If on the face of it, it seemed that suffering, injustice, and death had the last word over goodness, love, and life, now they knew the opposite was true.

> *Faith…is not a leap in the dark so much as a step into the light.*

Faith is believing against appearances. But it's not a leap in the dark so much as a step into the light. A letter attributed to Peter written after Jesus' resurrection puts it this way:

> Blessed be the God and Father of Our Lord Jesus Christ, who in his great mercy gave us a new birth to a living hope through the resurrection of Jesus Christ from the dead to an inheritance that is imperishable, undefiled and unfading, kept in heaven for you who by the power of God are safeguarded through faith to a salvation that is ready to be revealed in the final time. In this you rejoice, although now for a little while you may have to suffer various trials….Although you have not seen him you love him and without seeing you now believe in him, and rejoice with an indescribable joy, touched with glory because you are achieving faith's goal, your salvation. (1 Peter 1:3–6, 8)

Jesus' disciples had heard him speak often and fondly of his Father. One day Phillip said to Jesus, "show us the Father." Jesus replied that in knowing him they already knew what the Father was like. Jesus is what God looks like when God comes into our world, our history, and our lives.

Now that Jesus is risen, he is as truly present to you as he was to his followers when he was alive. He is the same person who said and did the things they saw and heard. Now you can talk to him about those same things, just as they did.

There is so much to talk about. Everything beautiful you have experienced, every tender moment, every sacrifice made from love, every act of courage, of endurance, of reaching out, everything that is precious to you has been made worthwhile forever, by him who made your *life* worthwhile forever.

By turning to the gospel accounts of Matthew, Mark, Luke, and John, you can enter each scene in Jesus' life. This involves using your imagination, but it is not mere fantasy; it is really happening because Jesus is really present to you. The events of his life become a catalyst for what is taking place in *your* life.

Make your own some of the questions and the requests that the people in the gospels asked of Jesus. You will be praying with a sense of how he responded to them, and responds to you. No one ever came away from Jesus with less than they had asked for.

# For Practice

• Spend some quiet time reflecting on the following passage. Use your imagination to put yourself in the scene with Jesus.

*As the sun was setting, all those who had any who were sick with various kinds of diseases brought them to him; and he laid his hands on each of them and cured them....At daybreak he departed and went into a deserted place. And the crowds were looking for him; and when they reached him, they wanted to prevent him from leaving them. But he said to them, "I must proclaim the good news of the kingdom of God to the other cities also; for I was sent for this purpose." So he continued proclaiming the message in the synagogues of Judea. (Luke 4:40, 42–44)*

• What might Jesus have said to you if you had had a few minutes with him that evening?

# For Prayer

Here comes with power the Lord God,
    who rules by his strong arm;
    here is his reward with him,
    his recompense before him.
Like a shepherd he feeds his flock;
    in his arms he gathers the lambs,
    carrying them in his bosom,
    and leading the ewes with care.
                 *Isaiah 40:10–12*

# 10 Salvation History Continued

You weren't there with those who knew Jesus during his lifetime. But you were included, because the key to understanding the Christian faith is *presence*—the real presence of Jesus among his followers after his resurrection, until the end of time.

> ...the message which was a hidden mystery from generations and centuries and has now been revealed to his holy ones....The mystery is Christ among you, your hope of glory. (Colossians 1:26, 27)

Through his resurrection he has passed into a new kind of existence that is not limited by time and place. He lives his life "in us":

> ...the life I live now is not my own; Christ is living in me. I still live my human life, but it is a life of faith in the Son of God, who loved me and gave himself for me. (Galatians 2:19, 20)

His life in us shows itself in ways that are reminiscent of Jesus of Nazareth:

> In the community called Christian,
> I find people of flesh and blood
>     and ordinary lives
> living in expectation of meeting You,
> undefeated by their personal failures
>     and by death itself.
> I have watched their faces in quiet prayer
>     and in songs of joy;
> I have felt humbled no less by their repentance
>     than by their faithfulness;
> I have known their sacrifices,
> been empowered by their serenity
> and learned the reason for the hope
>     that is in them.
> Their sureness is not based
>     on any success of their own

> but on what they believe
>     You have done for them.
> There is power in what they seem to know,
> and all the more striking
>     because human nature is so weak.

> I thank you, Father, for having revealed
>     great things to little ones.
> In the community of those who live
> now not they but Christ living in them,
> I have seen frail human nature raised up
> reaching heights of hope and depths of peace
> which nothing in the world could give nor,
>     it seems, take away.
> In their midst I come to know
> that he who enabled the lame to walk
>     and the blind to see
>     and sinners to start again
> is risen,
> for that is what their lives proclaim.
> And so I believe in Him in whom
>     they have placed their trust.
>         P.J. Cullinane, *I Believe Within the Church*

Whenever we see him like this, our faith in him is fresh again; re-freshed! It's a bit like being at the tomb on Easter morning. After all, his resurrection cannot grow old, and his presence is now.

Jesus had told his disciples that they would see these signs of his power:

> In all truth I tell you, whoever believes in me will perform the same works as I do myself, and will perform even greater works, because I am going to the Father. (John 14:12)

These "works" are what Jesus meant when he spoke about God's "kingdom" as something "already present"—visible to those who have eyes for recognizing the style of Jesus of Nazareth.

This kingdom is not some kind of place. It is God's saving power showing itself in people's lives—God's reign in our lives; salvation history continued. It shows in the kind of things that make you feel glad or deeply moved—sacrifices people make for others in need; the smiles of those who have been suffering; reconciliation between individuals who had hurt each other; the joys of faith and of faithfulness, of belonging and of being forgiven; and the beauty of truth itself—of whatever rings true.

Seeing God's saving power often causes surprise, especially if we were not expecting to find it in our own life. Those moments when you know that what God wants is also what you yourself most deeply want, even if it is demanding; or when you experience a joy you can't fully account for; or when you know with deep certainty that you can trust God; or you find yourself thanking God in spite of the darkness around you—all those moments are signs of God's real presence in your own life. They lead to wonder, joy, thanksgiving, and trust. They bring life.

To see God in this way is to come alive. Your relationship with God is what makes your life more truly human. It isn't added to a fully human life. It makes life more fully human.

> The glory of God is human beings fully alive, and being fully alive is (comes from) seeing God. (St. Irenaeus)

## For Practice

• Identify some signs of Christ's presence in people you know.

• Jesus often healed people and told them their faith had made them whole. Practice keeping the company of Jesus as someone you have complete faith in. Bring to him experiences that have left you hurt and in need of healing. Talk to him about them, and let him talk to you. Then leave it all to him.

## For Prayer

Sing a new song to the Lord
    who has done marvelous deeds,
    whose right hand and holy arm
    have brought salvation.

All the ends of the earth have seen
    the salvation of our God.
Shout to the Lord all the earth,
    ring out your joy.

Let the sea and what fills it resound,
    the world, and all its peoples.
Let the rivers clap their hands
    and the hills ring out their joy,

Before the Lord who comes
    who comes to govern the earth,
    to govern the world with justice
    and the peoples with fairness.

*Psalm 98:1, 3–4, 7–9*

# 11  Your Future

If you had asked the apostle Paul to say who you are he probably would not have looked to your origins and your past, but to your future. After all, who you will be eventually is a statement about who you are now. "What we shall be" really excited Paul and those first Christians. For Paul, our sharing in the risen Christ's life was so real that he could say we have been "raised up and given a place with him in heaven" (Ephesians 2:6).

It is our present lives that are different because of this. Think of those moments when you have looked out on the world and experienced profoundly and intimately the joy of being alive; or glimpsed the beauty of nature, the love of a friend, the bonds of family, or the marvel and mystery of life itself. It's precisely these things—and therefore our present lives—that would be empty and futile if in the end they come to nothing. Trying to live with that, and powerless to make any difference, is what Scripture calls the "crippling power" of death.

That is precisely what Jesus' resurrection changes. He hasn't exempted us from the experience of death; he has destroyed its power over us. He has turned it around on itself, changing it from being the end of our hopes to being the reason for our hope. Everything and everyone dear to us has been restored to us; every joy, love, and hope has become worthwhile and purposeful and wonderful, because so is our future.

> *By rising from the dead, Christ has taken our human nature, made from this creation, into a glorified existence. The whole of creation, through its union with Christ, is now linked with the life of God.*

The whole of creation is being re-created, and it is God's doing:

> Then I saw a new heaven and a new earth. The former heaven and the former earth had passed away, and the sea was no more. I also saw the holy city, the new Jerusalem, coming down out of heaven from God, prepared as a bride adorned for her husband. I heard a loud voice from the throne saying, "Behold, God's dwelling is with the human race. He will dwell with them and they will be his people and God himself will always be with them. He will wipe every tear from their eyes, and there shall be no more death or mourning, wailing or pain, for the old order has passed away." The one who sat on the throne said, "Behold, I make all things new."…He went on to say: these words are already fulfilled. (Revelation 21:1–6)

Christ, in person, is the new creation, and we become part of that new creation through our union with him. At his conception he became, forever, united to the created world. By rising from the dead, Christ has taken our human nature, made from this creation, into a glorified existence. The whole of creation, through its union with Christ, is now linked with the life of God.

> Let us give thanks to the Father for having made you worthy to share the lot of the saints in light. He rescued us from the power of darkness and brought us into the kingdom of his beloved son. Through him we have redemp-

tion, the forgiveness of our sins. He is the image of the invisible God, the first-born of all creatures. In him everything in heaven and on earth was created, things visible and invisible. All were created through him; all were created for him; he is before all else that is. In him everything continues in being. It is he who is the head of the body, the Church. He who is the beginning, the first-born of the dead, so that primacy may be his in everything. It pleased God to make absolute fullness reside in him. And, by means of him, to reconcile everything in his person, both on earth and in the heavens, making peace through the blood of his cross. (Colossians 1:12–20)

Living the Christian life means putting into practice your identity as someone already "raised up and given a place with Christ in heaven." You do this not by being "other-worldly" in a way that makes you indifferent to the world around you, but by bringing your true dignity to bear on the world around you and letting it make all the difference. When the time comes for your "mortal nature to put on immortality," this will be the time for you to live more deeply than ever! Just as your life was a gift and a calling in the first place; and just as being united to the risen Christ is a gift and a calling, so, too, passing into everlasting life is a gift and a calling, not something we can just take or demand.

To wait for your death is to wait upon the One who wants you to have everlasting life, but never owed it to you. So we await it as we would await a gift. Death is the threshold we cross over, when called. Waiting is the time for living this important part of our journey, in union with Christ and with the confidence this gives us. This is to die with dignity.

## For Practice

• Reflect on the saying "they live more fully who are not afraid to die." What would your life be like for you if you never knew God had a future for you?

• Think of what you might want to say to God when your place in God's plan has been fully and finally revealed to you. Is it something you might want to say now?

## For Prayer

Age to age shall proclaim your works,
    shall declare your awesome deeds
    shall speak of your splendor and glory,
    tell the tale of your mighty works.
They will speak of your fearsome deeds,
    recount your greatness and might.
They will recall your abundant goodness;
    and joyfully sing of justice.

The Lord is kind and full of compassion,
    slow to anger, abounding in love.
How good is the Lord to all,
    compassionate to every creature....

The Lord is trustworthy in every word,
    and faithful in every work.
The Lord supports all who call
    and raises up all who are bowed down.
*Psalm 145:4–9, 13–14*

# 12 No One Is an Island

Your relationship with God is obviously personal: no one can take your place in the history of the universe. And God's love for you is personal. But personal doesn't mean private.

The culture in which we live makes much of "the individual." That's a word that says nothing about your relationship with others. Being a person, on the other hand, means being in relationship to others. The difference this makes is huge, so let's think about it.

Our culture tends to talk about important things like truth and freedom in terms of the individual. For example, truth is often described as whatever the individual believes it is. It's "true" for him or her. This reduces truth to mere opinion. Right and wrong are described in terms of "individual choice." It is even claimed that "no one can judge"; no one else can say what is right or wrong for "the individual." "Freedom" is described as the right to do whatever an individual chooses.

So where does that leave us when an individual thinks it is right to fly a plane into an office building, if "no one else can judge"? Or when lives are terminated through abortion or assisted suicide because "the individual has the right to choose"?

But do right and wrong, true and false, depend entirely on the individual? And do we really want a society in which individuals are accountable only to themselves?

If truth is ultimately only a matter of each individual's opinion, and if right is whatever the individual chooses, then the very possibility of dialogue, public debate, and consensus is ruled out before it can start. Individualism ultimately puts us beyond each other's reach. It cuts across our deep human need to belong to, and with, one another.

Individualism fails to recognize that we can only really be ourselves in relation to others, and through being for others. Promoting self independently of others is promoting a false self. This shows up in the fact that when everybody "minds their own business," individuals are more vulnerable, more isolated, and more lonely than ever. People are suffering because of this. It is unnatural. Ultimately, it is unlivable.

*When everybody "minds their own business," individuals are more vulnerable, more isolated, and more lonely than ever.*

This is probably why some people are now looking for ways to reconnect with everything, and often through nature. But nature religions, even those of a new age, cannot ultimately deliver what is needed (see chapter 6).

## For Practice

• Take notice of how prevalent individualism is in our culture today. You can observe this through the media as well as in your interactions with others. What are some of the ways that you can promote a more communal approach to life? Why would this be valuable today?

# For Prayer

Trust in the Lord and do good
    that you may dwell in the land and live secure.
Find your delight in the Lord
    who will give you your heart's desire.
Commit your life to the Lord;
    trust in God and God will act.

Those whose steps are guided by the Lord,
    whose way God approves,
    may stumble, but they will never fall,
    for the Lord holds their hand.
The salvation of the just is from the Lord,
    their refuge in time of distress.
The Lord helps and rescues them
    from the wicked,
    for they take refuge in the Lord.

*Psalm 37:3–5, 23–24, 39–40*

UNLESS THERE IS SOME OBJECTIVE BASIS for determining what is right and wrong, right and wrong end up being whatever the individual wants or believes. That objective basis is the meaning that belongs to things, rather than the meanings we give them.

Some actions mean what we want them to mean; for example, a handshake can mean greeting someone or sympathizing or clinching a deal. But there are other things that already have a meaning that doesn't depend on us, or on circumstances. Take the biological differences between male and female: these differences don't tell us everything about the meaning of sexuality, but they do tell us something about its purpose and meaning. To fly in the face of meaning is to fly in the face of reality.

Whenever meaning is already written into nature, it is not our intentions that give meaning. That's why a person might even do a right action for a wrong reason, or a wrong action with good intentions. Nor is it enough to claim that we are being "loving" or following our natural inclinations. People involved in fornication, adultery, or homosexuality could all claim they are being loving and following their natural inclinations. The point is: are their actions consistent with the meaning of sexuality and the meaning of marriage? Nor do right and wrong depend only on the consequences of our actions. Adultery is still wrong even if it isn't found out and no one gets hurt in any obvious sense. Even good consequences aren't enough to justify wrong actions; for example, the desire to have a healthy baby can't justify every means of getting one, much less the "termination" of other embryos.

Of course, it is part of our calling as human beings to take responsibility for and shape our world and our lives. But does this mean we have unlimited dominion over our lives and the world, or do we have only a limited dominion? Do all things have only the meaning that we put on them, or do some things have a meaning that is independent of our choices? Is human nature whatever we can make it into, using new technology, with no pre-set limits to what is human? Or, does being human have a meaning already written into it that we need to respect?

# 13 In the Marketplace

Are you in danger of being used, or of using others? In the context of social and economic life, individualism translates as the economic survival of the fittest. That represents a kind of diminishment, not only for those at the bottom of the heap, but also for those who put them there.

People are thought of as "units" in the industrial process, a kind of "human capital." They are thought of as producers and consumers, to be factored in or factored out depending on the needs of the market. The consequences can be shattering for people's sense of self-worth, their marriage and family. The joy of living can be crushed out of them. It is dehumanizing because

*Solidarity…means that you are incomplete so long as others are incomplete.*

> …there are collective and qualitative needs which cannot be satisfied by market mechanisms. There are important human needs which escape its logic. There are goods which by their nature cannot and must not be sold. (Pope John Paul II, *Centesimus Annus*)

There are subtle ways of giving things priority over persons—ways that already infiltrate society's thinking. For example, those who contribute their labor to an enterprise are putting into it something genuinely personal. Those who contribute financial capital, perhaps through a broker, are providing something impersonal. Yet it is commonly assumed that those who provide financial capital are entitled to a greater say in the management of industry and to a greater share in its profits than those who provide their labor!

Whenever persons are subordinated to other values it is through failure to recognize that persons have a worth and dignity that transcends their usefulness and their circumstances. This transcendent value of each person is ultimately based on how much each person matters to God. God's own statement on how much each person matters is the life, death, and resurrection of Christ.

Every person is sacred to God from the first moment of their existence, in all the situations of their life, through their dying, and forever. This includes the person that others call "you."

If there were no transcendent basis for human dignity, then the well-being of persons would depend on their resourcefulness and their circumstances and on how much society can do to protect them. And if religious faith is a purely "private" affair, then it can't help them either. This is why the

> …split between the faith which many profess and their daily lives deserves to be counted among the more serious errors of our age. (Second Vatican Council, *Church in the World*)

The connection between religious faith and the rest of life is implicitly acknowledged by those who want to keep "religion" inside the Church so that it doesn't get in the way of their social and economic agendas.

Of course, religious faith does not substitute for the proper dynamics of social and economic planning. But it is religious faith that gives us the reason why persons are meant to be the *goal* of social and economic planning and not a mere means to other goals.

> I would like to invite economists and financial professionals, as well as political leaders, to recognize the urgency of the need to ensure that economic practices and related political policies have as their aim the good of every person and of the whole person. This is not only a demand of ethics but also of a sound economy. Experience seems to confirm that economic success is increasingly dependent on a more genuine appreciation of individuals and their abilities, on their fuller participation, on their increased and improved knowledge and information, on a stronger solidarity. (Pope John Paul II, message on the World Day of Peace, 1 January 2000)

The opposite of individualism is solidarity. It means accepting that the well-being of each is connected with the well-being of all. It means that you are incomplete so long as others are incomplete. It can also mean that if you are not part of the solution you are part of the problem. You become your true self through your being in some way "for others."

Is it just a coincidence that those who are most universally admired—regardless of particular beliefs—are those who have transcended themselves—"losing" their lives for others?

# For Practice

• Identify someone in the business community whom you respect, and reflect on why you respect them.

• Some businesses take social and environmental impact into consideration in their policies and practices. Others argue that those issues are the concern of governments, and that the business of business is business, that is, making money. What do you think?

# For Prayer

The law of the Lord is perfect,
  it revives the soul.
The rule of the Lord is trustworthy,
  it gives wisdom to the simple.
The precepts of the Lord are right,
  they gladden the heart.
The command of the Lord is clear,
  it gives light to the eyes.
The fear of the Lord is holy,
  abiding for ever.
The decrees of the Lord are true,
  all of them just.

*Psalm 19:7–9*

# 14 You and the Common Good

So what is the role of government? If the dignity of every person really is paramount, then the proper role of government is to create the social and economic conditions that maximize each person's opportunity to pursue their personal fulfillment. That kind of environment is called the *common good*.

The common good is not a matter of subordinating individuals to some kind of collective value, or of subordinating minority interests to majority interests. Nor is it a matter of flattening out people's opportunities to some kind of highest common factor.

The common good is about persons and each person's access to the kind of living conditions (e.g., housing, health, employment, education, and access to resources) that enables them to make meaningful decisions for their own lives and contribute to the lives of others. That kind of environment requires some measure of regulation. Otherwise, the "freedom" of some and "free-market" conditions become the oppression of others.

But government intervention must also respect the dignity of persons by exercising only a *subsidiary* role in their lives. It is not for higher authorities to do what groups and individual people can properly do for themselves. It belongs to our human dignity to take responsibility, as much as possible, for the direction of our own lives. Moreover, it is individual people and voluntary groups who bring passion and commitment to the causes they espouse. It is for government to actively encourage and enable local initiatives.

The common good and solidarity are inclusive of all, in ever-wider circles:

...there will be peace only to the extent that humanity as a whole rediscovers its fundamental calling to be one family, a family in which the dignity and rights of every person, whatever their status, race, or religion, are accepted as prior and superior to any kind of difference or distinction.

This recognition can give the world as it is today—marked by the process of globalization—a soul, a meaning, and a direction. Globalization, for all its risks, also offers exceptional and promising opportunities, precisely with a view to enabling humanity to become a single family, built on the values of justice, equity, and solidarity.

For this to happen, a complete change of perspective will be needed: it is no longer the well-being of any one political, racial, or cultural community that must prevail, but rather the good of humanity as a whole. The pursuit of the common good of a single political community cannot be in conflict with the common good of humanity, expressed in the recognition of and respect for human rights sanctioned by the Universal Declaration of Human Rights of 1948. It is necessary, then, to abandon ideas and practices, often determined by powerful economic interests, which subordinate every other value to the absolute claims of the nation and the state. In this new perspective, the political, cultural and institutional divisions and distinctions by which humanity is ordered and organized are legitimate in so far as they are compatible with membership in the one human family. (Pope John Paul II, message on the World Day of Peace, 1 January 2000)

Personal fulfillment and the common good are not competing concepts that need to be balanced against each other; they are part of each other. It isn't the common good if it doesn't aim to include what you need to be able to exercise personal choice and responsibility. And it isn't your personal fulfillment if it doesn't include your commitment to the common good.

But what chance is there of solidarity in a world bent on individualistic self-interest? We shall return to this question in a later chapter.

## For Practice

- Can you identify examples of government involvement that discourages or inhibits personal or local initiative?
- Can you identify examples of government non-involvement when the common good requires it?
- What do you feel is your responsibility in promoting the common good? How do you go about this in your daily life?

## For Prayer (for those who govern)

O God, give your judgement to the king;
    that he may govern your people with justice,
    your oppressed with right judgement,
that the mountains may yield their bounty
    for the people,
    and the hills abundance,
that he may defend the oppressed
      among the people,
    save the poor and crush the oppressor.

May he be like rain coming down upon the fields,
    like showers watering the earth.

For he shall save the poor when they cry
    and the needy who are helpless.
He will have pity on the weak
    and save the lives of the poor.
*Psalm 72:1–4, 6, 12–13*

# 15 Your Share of the Earth

What does being "at home" mean for you? How big is your home? Solidarity with all the peoples of the earth involves reverence for the earth itself, on which we all depend for our lives. The well-being of people and the well-being of the earth are interdependent.

When the planet is abused, human life and human well-being are diminished. When, for example, a small fraction of the world's population possesses and consumes most of the world's resources while larger numbers of the population suffer undernourishment and even starvation, the world and its people are being abused. The same is true when scarce resources are ravaged and depleted, and even the most basic resources such as air and water are being polluted.

> The protection of the environment is not only a technical question; it is also and above all an ethical issue. (Pope John Paul II, *Letter to the Church in Asia*)

Wrong relationships with creation constitute a wrong relationship with the Creator. So,

> What is needed is an act of repentance on our part and a renewed attempt to view ourselves, one another, and the world around us within the divine design for creation. The problem is not simply economic and technological; it is moral and spiritual. A solution at the economic and technological level can be found only if we undergo, in the most radical way, an inner change of heart, which can lead to a change of lifestyle and sustainable patterns of consumption and production. (From a dialogue between Pope John Paul II and Patriarch Bartholomew of Constantinople, June 2002)

Even management of resources involves something more than management; it depends on how we view the natural world.

One way is to see the natural world mainly as a resource to meet our material needs. Those who control the resources spare no effort in persuading people to buy more, possess more, and consume more, not stopping at real needs but including mere wants. Consumerism becomes the goal of economic activity.

To meet the demand, resources are exploited as fully as possible. This is what leads to the pollution and depletion of resources, and the amassing of people into overcrowded centers of population so that more natural resources can be exploited. This way of consuming resources is relatively recent in human history, and characteristically Western.

A much older approach, common to many indigenous peoples, also sees the natural world as a resource for meeting material needs, but sees it mainly as the environment in which we meet a wider range of human needs. Humans do not live by bread alone; the natural world also nourishes our spirits. It is where we most easily experience beauty and wonder; where we can "be still and know God."

Preserving the planet's ability to be a true "home" for the nurture of our spirits as well as

*Humans do not live by bread alone; the natural world also nourishes our spirits.*

our bodies requires that the exploitation of resources be on the basis of the *minimum* necessary for our real needs.

The lands, forests, fisheries, rivers, and "treasures" which the Treaty of Waitangi seeks to protect for the "undisturbed possession" of the Maori people cannot be understood merely in terms of material needs; they are first and foremost the home or environment in which people meet their spiritual needs.

Underlying this view of the natural world is a sense of it being
- a gift
- that is reverenced because it is received from the Creator
- and over which we exercise not so much ownership as stewardship;

Because creation was entrusted to human stewardship, the natural world is not just a resource to be exploited but also a reality to be respected and even reverenced as a gift and trust from God. It is the task of human beings to care for, preserve, and cultivate the treasures of creation (Pope John Paul II, *Letter to the Church in Oceania*).

# For Practice

- Look at photographs of people who are suffering from poverty, hunger, loneliness, or war. Reflect on why this is happening to them. Then ask yourself whether you benefit from any of the political or economic arrangements that contribute to their suffering.

- Read the prophet Amos 8:1–12 to get a sense of how the earth, and we ourselves, wither up when we try to live by bread alone.

# For Prayer

You keep pledge with wonders,
   O God our savior,
     the hope of all the earth
     and of far distant isles.
By your strength you
     established the mountains;
     you are girded with might.
You still the roaring of the seas,
     the roaring of the waves
     and the tumult of the peoples.
The ends of the earth stand in awe
     at the sight of your wonders.
The lands of sunrise and sunset
     you fill with your joy.
You care for the earth, give it water,
     you fill it with riches.
Your river in heaven brims over
     to provide its grain.
And so you provide for the earth;
     you drench its furrows,
     you level it, soften it with showers,
     you bless its growth.
You crown the year with your goodness.
Abundance flows in your steps,
     in the pastures of the wilderness it flows.
The hills are girded with joy,
     the meadows covered with flocks,
     the valleys are decked with wheat.
They shout for joy, yes, they sing.

*Psalm 65:5–13*

# 16 Body/Person

How does your body belong to who you really are? It reveals your presence. It is your person that is bodily present to others, and as such, your body shares the dignity of your person.

It is through our bodies that we reach one another. Through the eyes of others we see ourselves. What a child or youth or ex-prison inmate sees in another's eyes can make or break their chances in life. When they look to you for a sign of their own worth, do they see someone who believes in them (still) or doesn't, or who leaves them not knowing? Have you ever noticed that little look of disappointment in a child's eyes when some over-careful adult, out of fear of being misjudged, denied the child the palpable sign of affection it was innocently looking for?

It is through our bodies that we find intimacy. Being male or female is not additional to being a person. It is the way you *are* a person. Sexuality is nature's first hint that we become ourselves through being "for others." This is symbolized especially in the marriage relationship. The Catholic Church teaches that marriage is a sacrament; in other words, God's own life-giving, self-giving, love for the husband and wife is made *present* to them—em-bodied—in their love for each other. Christian marriage is intended to mirror the completeness of Christ's love for us:

> This is my body (my self) given up for you…my blood (my life) poured out for you. (Luke 22:19–20)

> It is your person that is bodily present to others, and as such, your body shares the dignity of your person.

Sexual differentiation and complementarity are part of the "language" that points to our destiny as a communion of persons sharing the same wonderful life.

When human sexuality is turned from being an expression of self-giving into an expression of grasping and possessing, the other is being treated not as a person to be loved, but as an object to be used. You are a gift to others—your true self—only when you treat others as persons.

Self-respect, respect for others, and self-control make for chastity. A society that makes light of chastity and winks at pornography in the name of freedom brings on itself precisely those behaviors that involve lack of self-respect, lack of respect for others, and lack of self-control. Society's confusion about sexuality has consequences beyond sexuality itself.

From her experience of New Zealand prisons, Celia Lashlie found that "the attitudes held by many male offenders towards women…often lay at the heart of the reasons why they were in prison" (*The Journey to Prison*). Can society be serious about reducing sexual abuse and domestic violence if it believes that sexual self-indulgence is "harmless," and that expecting self-control (chastity) is unrealistic? Chastity matters because persons matter. It is about treating yourself and others as persons, not as objects to be exploited, dominated, or trivialized.

The human community to which we are linked

through our bodies includes not only our contemporaries, but the generations before us. Each of us has an historical context, a story, that goes back to before we were born. Your way of being you is linked to the ways of your ancestors.

A people's "ways" are their culture. Culture is not something people can pick up or put down. Our ancestors are our roots, and we are their shoots, branches, and blossoms. Cut off from our culture, we are cut off from our natural ways of being ourselves. Respect for persons includes respect for their culture, the "ways" that are culturally natural to them.

Cultures can also be de-humanizing and not life-giving. Every culture needs to be purified. As Christ's gospel gradually changes our selves, it transforms our relationships, our "ways," and society. It touches all that is human. But "there is no new humanity if there are not first of all new persons" (Pope Paul VI, *Letter on Evangelization*).

Sometimes the body has been given a bad name, through a misunderstanding of what Scripture means by "spiritual"—as if the body gets in the way of our spiritual relationship with God. But in the writings of Paul, your "spiritual" self is your whole self (body and soul) when your life is turned towards God. And it is your whole self (soul as well as body) that is "unspiritual" when your life is turned away from God.

God, too, is revealed through the human body. The incarnation is the invisible God being made visible. "The Word was made flesh and dwelt among us" (John 1:14).

We come to be aware of God in ways that are natural to us as human persons. The sights, sounds, and smells associated with the places and times of Christian rites and ceremonies, feast days, devotions, and decorations deeply impact our consciousness, creating a sense of what it's like to be who we are. It is your whole self (body as much as soul) that you put into your worship when you participate in the postures, gestures, stillness, movements, words, songs, and silences of the whole community acting as "one body, one spirit, in Christ." And it is your whole person—body, mind, and spirit—that will be glorified.

My heart is glad, my soul rejoices; even my body shall rest in hope. (Psalm 16)

# For Practice

• Cultural and ethnic differences can make us more aware of the humanity we have in common, and of each individual's uniqueness in the whole of creation. Try becoming more aware of this when you are close to others, especially those who are "strangers."

# For Prayer

To your eyes a thousand years
    are like yesterday, come and gone,
    no more than a watch in the night.
You sweep us mortals away like a dream,
    like grass which springs up in the morning.
In the morning it springs up and flowers:
    by evening it withers and fades…

Our span is seventy years
    or eighty for those who are strong.…

Make us know the shortness of our life
    that we may gain wisdom of heart.
*Psalm 90:4–6, 10, 12*

# Part II

Turning towards God is a way of life—your spiritual life. It develops, unfolds, and grows. People spend time and money developing their personality, appearances, and relating skills, for the sake of what others see. But what about the person who is you even when no one sees you? The following chapters are about developing that person, and the kind of person you will be for others.

# 17 Responding to God in Your Life

God's first word to you called you into existence. Living your life is your response to that call: you become what you and God do together. Your life is a gift; it is also a task and a responsibility.

But your life is not an imposition. Your own deepest and best longings were part of what God chose when God chose you. So being true to your best self and being true to God are the same thing. In that sense, your relationship with God is not a burden. God's "law" is within you.

> O God, you are my God, for you I long;
>    for you my soul is thirsting.
> My body pines for you
>    like a dry, weary land without water.
> So I gaze on you in the sanctuary
>    to see your strength and your glory.
> For your love is better than life,
>    my lips will speak your praise.
> So I will bless you all my life,
>    in your name I will lift up my hands.
>
> My soul shall be filled as with a banquet,
>    my mouth shall praise you with joy.
> On my bed I remember you.
> On you I muse through the night
>    for you have been my help;
>    in the shadow of your wings I rejoice.
> My soul clings to you;
>    your right hand holds me fast.
>
> *Psalm 63:1–8*

Knowing God's will for you, and knowing yourself result from being close to each other, in

*Imagine yourself at the far end of your life and looking back. The choices that will give you the most gladness then are the choices that are right for you now.*

the way that friends know each other. It involves talking to God and knowing that you are heard; listening, being faithful, and being in tune with your true self:

> Be transformed by the renewal of your mind so that you may discern what is the will of God. (Romans 12:2)

An ancient Christian saying puts it this way: when you love, then you will understand.

The conversation involves your core self, but it is not hidden inside you. Your talents are part of the conversation—they tell you something about God's hopes for you.

God also speaks to you in the circumstances of your life. These include what the world around you most needs from you. The place where God calls you is the place "where your deep gladness meets the world's deep needs" (Frederick Buechner). Even people's human rights can have no meaning unless others have a duty to meet those rights. What is a right to food if no one has the duty to provide it? By actively seeking opportunities to meet the needs of others you are living out the dialogue you have with God, even when you are not explicitly thinking of God.

This dialogue involves making decisions and choices. Sometimes the options in front of you are big and sometimes they are small, for example, when we choose between putting a little more kindness into the world or putting less kindness; more honesty or less honesty; more forgiveness or less forgiveness, and so on. Every good choice builds up an environment in which bolder steps become possible. The world was meant to be different because of you. You, too, are different because of the choices you make. We become as we do.

Sometimes we have to choose between options that are all good. When you come to a cross-roads—when choosing one direction excludes other options—don't get paralyzed by trying to keep all your options open! Freedom and fulfillment and peace of mind come through decision and commitment, not through trying to keep all options open.

Whether it is a big choice or just a little one, you can sometimes know which is the right choice by imagining yourself at the far end of your life and looking back. The choices that will give you the most gladness then are the choices that are right for you now.

God's "yes" to you and your "yes" to God come together in the person of Jesus (see 2 Corinthians 1:19–20). Christ both inspires your response through the gospels, and enables your response through his life in you.

> After those days, says the Lord, I will place my law within them, and write it upon their hearts; I will be their God, and they will be my people. (Jeremiah 31:33)

In surrendering to God, we discover God.

# For Practice

- Think of some decision you have made that you will be glad about at the end of your life.

# For Prayer

To you, O Lord, I lift up my soul
I trust you, let me not be disappointed….

Lord, make me know your ways,
    teach me your paths.
Guide me in your truth, and teach me:
    for you are God my savior.

Good and upright is the Lord,
    who shows sinners the way,
    guides the humble in the right path,
    and teaches the poor the way.
*Psalm 25:1–2, 4–5, 8–9*

# 18 The Journey into Reality

Becoming the person you are called to be is a journey into reality. This journey involves shedding all that is not your true self: the masks, the excuses, the self-deceptions and illusions, the false ambitions and escape routes, the fears, pretenses, and prejudices, and anything that makes you its slave. The deep longings you still experience when you are most free of everything that lacks authenticity are the longings God created in creating you.

The journey is about becoming more real. That's the joy of it: you never have to pretend to be anything or anyone that you are not! There is great freedom in being your true self. But it presupposes that you make judgments that distinguish between true and false.

There are subtle ways we avoid the journey; for example, by keeping ourselves too busy to think about unresolved issues. Chasing after passing fashions or acquiring more things can serve as a distraction; keeping rigidly to a narrow routine can also be a way of avoiding whatever else there might be to see. Looking for ready-made, authoritative answers (fundamentalism) rather than going more deeply into the questions is also a way of avoiding the journey into reality.

There will be mistakes on this journey; perfection is at the end of the journey, not before. Part of accepting reality is accepting yourself, including your track record and your failures.

Does this mean there is no need for change? No, it means that important change takes place when we accept what we are (which includes our frailty and failures) rather than try to be what we are not (i.e., someone who doesn't have any frailties or failures). So we need a way of dealing with frailty and failure that doesn't involve denying them. This is why knowing about God's forgiveness and acceptance makes all the difference. To know that God has accepted Christ's faithfulness in place of our unfaithfulness is what makes Christian faith a great privilege:

> If God is for us, who can be against us? God did not spare even his own son…how will he not also give us everything else along with him? Who will bring a charge against those God acquits? Who will condemn? It is Christ…who intercedes for us. (Romans 8:31–34)

We need to accept that the journey is gradual. Otherwise we might try to compensate for not being better than we actually are. Compensating can lead to an unhealthy perfectionism (the feeling that you have to make everything "right"), or to disillusionment (discovering that you can't).

The starting point for this journey is always the present moment, whatever its circumstances. There is no other time—we cannot be in the past or in the future. So you never have to wait until you are in better circumstances or in "a better space." To postpone meeting God is to avoid God, and to avoid God is to avoid the self that comes about from "seeing" God.

God meets you in the reality of your own life.

*You never have to pretend to be anything or anyone that you are not.*

There is no other place for you to meet God. This seems so obvious. Yet isn't this the truth we miss when we imagine we could really meet God if we were like someone else, or better prepared, or more worthy? God is saying to us: "Come as you are…."

# For Practice

• Slowly pray Psalm 23. As you pray, let your mind rest on the images found in these words.

The Lord is my shepherd;
    there is nothing I shall want.
Fresh and green are the pastures
    where you give me repose.

Near restful waters you lead me,
    to restore my strength.
You guide me along the right path;
You are true to your name.

If I should walk in the valley of darkness
    no evil would I fear.
You are there with your crook and your staff;
    with these you give me comfort.

You have prepared a banquet for me
    in the sight of my foes.
My head you have anointed with oil;
    my cup is overflowing.

Surely goodness and kindness shall follow me
    all the days of my life.
In the Lord's own house shall I dwell
    for ever and ever.

# 19 Keeping in Touch

**B**ring your body along with you. Rather, let it bring you. The journey into reality is the journey towards becoming fully human and fully alive from "seeing" God. We cannot do this in an abstract or theoretical way. It has to be real. This is why our bodily senses are so important on this journey.

Our intellect enables us to understand the information that comes to us through our senses. We analyze, make inferences, and draw conclusions. We plan and give direction to our work. Our intellect makes all this possible. Intellectual understanding is part of being human and being alive.

*The delight we find in beauty or goodness of any kind is a window through which we see God.*

But intellectual understanding is abstract. It is one step removed from the world that touches us through our senses. Isn't this what happens when the child who looks with wide-eyed wonder at a flapping, chirping bundle of warm flesh and feathers is given the generic name of what it sees; forever afterwards the child sees only "sparrows?"

Through your intellect you know *about* things; through your senses you *know* them. The journey into reality involves coming back to our senses:

> We must go back and start again with those five senses whose first messages to us in childhood were faultily decoded and then misunderstood. Then, they were heeded, ignored, edited or discarded to fit our small, subjective games. Now they must be given their true value, whether or not they suit our plans.
>
> These five senses remain our one certain link with the world outside us....We must first be prepared to waste our time. Away with the crowded schedule, itself a symptom of self-importance, a sign that we see ourselves as supermen. We must sacrifice a little time, surrendering to the senses, not thinking but feeling the world as it really is....
>
> We must watch the world, not to collect material, to utilize facts, to evolve theories, to propose and answer questions, but to become one with the world of senses through eye, ear, touch, taste and smell. One has but to undertake this exercise for ten minutes to grasp that the solution of our problems is at hand. The strain of life drains out with our self-importance when we mess in with the universe and abandon our individual pose. (Bernard Bassett, SJ, *The Noonday Devil*)

The delight we find in beauty or goodness of any kind is a window through which we see God. We look at a window in order to see through it. To look only at the glass is to miss the view. And so it is with God.

> To miss the transition from sensuous delight to a delight beyond the reach of our senses is to miss the upward movement of the inner life. Without the runway of the senses we could never take off. Yet, how shall we get airborne if we stick to the runway? In order to move through the senses to sense we must leave the senses behind....What our senses are after is sense. The goal of all our striving is meaning. Only in sense, in meaning, do our restless

hearts come to rest. (David Steindl-Rast, *A Listening Heart*)

Steindl-Rast uses the image of landscape and horizon to picture the relationship between senses and sense:

> Awareness of dying belongs to mindful living as the horizon belongs to the landscape. Death is the horizon of life's landscape; sense is the horizon of the landscape of the senses. The horizon lies always beyond; we can distinguish it from the landscape, but we cannot separate the two. The same is true of sense and the senses. Reject the senses, how will you find sense? Get stuck in the senses and life will be equally senseless.

There is paradox here: it is through being "in touch" that we transcend what we are in touch with. Sights and sounds vary in their ability to help us see God. There are pieces of music that lift us effortlessly to what lies behind their beauty. But we will miss both the beauty of the music and the beauty that it hints at if our environment is crowded out with noise. "Tuning in" means making choices and being selective. It calls for self-discipline and courage, even a sense of adventure.

Paul was being wonderfully inclusive and yet selective when he counseled the Philippians:

> Fill your minds with everything that is true, everything that is noble, everything that is good and pure, everything that we love and honor, and everything that can be thought virtuous or worthy of praise.(4:8)

# For Practice

• Enjoy beauty. Look at something beautiful. Listen to something beautiful. Go out and do something beautiful for somebody else.

# For Prayer

O give thanks to our God who is good:
  whose love endures forever.

You sun and moon, you stars of the southern sky:
  give to our God your thanks and praise.

Sunrise and sunset, night and day:
  give to our God your thanks and praise.

All mountains and valleys, grassland and scree,
  glacier, avalanche, mist and snow:
  give to our God your thanks and praise.

You kauri and pine, rata and kowhai,
  mosses and ferns:
  give to our God your thanks and praise.

Dolphins and kahawai, sea lion and crab,
  coral, anaemone, pipi and shrimp:
  give to our God your thanks and praise.

Rabbits and cattle, moths and dogs,
  kiwi and sparrow and tui and hawk:
  give to our God your thanks and praise.

You Maori and Pakeha, women and men,
  all who inhabit the long white cloud:
  give to our God your thanks and praise.

All you saints and martyrs of the South Pacific:
  give to our God your thanks and praise.

All prophets and priests, all cleaners and clerks,
  professors, shop workers, typists and teachers,
  job-seekers, invalids, drivers and doctors:
  give to our God your thanks and praise.

All sweepers and diplomats, writers and artists,
  grocers, carpenters, students and stock-agents,
  seafarers, farmers, bakers and mystics:
  give to our God your thanks and praise.

All children and infants, all people who play:
  give to our God your thanks and praise.

Benedicite Aotearoa, *A New Zealand Prayer Book: He Karakia Mihinare o Aotearoa*

# 20 The Heart of the Journey

Perhaps you won't be surprised to know that the core experience of journeying into reality is the same for you as it was for Jesus, who "pioneered" and "led the way" with his own journey (see the Letter to the Hebrews). Jesus is described as "learning obedience through suffering." He did not want to suffer, as suffering has no value in itself. It was simply the price he was prepared to pay for the sake of being faithful to his mission. He knew he could trust his Father even when his situation seemed hopeless.

In the strength that came from complete trust, he was able to surrender his life freely. And in return, his prayer was heard:

> During his life on earth, he offered up prayer and entreaty, aloud and in silent tears, to the One who had the power to save him out of death, and he submitted so humbly that his prayer was heard. Although he was Son, he learned to obey through suffering; and having been made perfect, he became for all who obey him, the source of eternal salvation. (Hebrews 5:7–9)

Growing in trust is the surest sign that we are journeying in the right direction. We move, gradually, from the wrong kind of self-sufficiency to reliance on the One who can still be trusted even when our situation is hopeless. Letting God be God is the most real thing we can do. Accepting our dependence on God is accepting our true selfhood.

When we open ourselves more to the power of God, our moments of greatest crisis become moments of greatest opportunity. At these times we can be like the climber being rescued from the face of a cliff who stubbornly holds on to the rock instead of letting himself fall into into the hands of the rescuers. We need to let go, entrust our whole self and life and destiny into the hands of the One who already has his arms around us in order to lift us to where we could never lift ourselves. It is when so much seems at stake that we most fear to let go, and have the most to gain by letting God be God. To trust God like that is to honor God; it is an act of worship.

> I love you, Lord, my strength,
>   my rock, my fortress, my saviour.
> My God is the rock where I take refuge;
>   my shield, my mighty help, my stronghold.
>
> You, O Lord, are my lamp,
>   my God who lightens my darkness.
> With you I can break through any barrier,
>   with my God I can scale any wall.
> *Psalm 18:1–2, 28–29*

Often it is through the experience of disappointment (when God does not meet our expectations) that we are brought further into reality, and to the realization that "God's ways are not our ways"—because they can only be better. For the apostle Paul, the struggle and the experience of human weakness gave scope to the power of Christ, and gave Paul his greatest joy:

> I have pleaded with the Lord three times for (this difficulty) to leave me, but he has said, "my grace is sufficient for you: my power is at

*Growing in trust is the surest sign that we are journeying in the right direction.*

its best in weakness." So I shall be very happy to make my weaknesses my special boast so that the power of Christ may stay over me, and that is why I am quite content with my weaknesses and with insults, hardships, persecutions, and the agonies I go through for Christ's sake. For it is when I am weak that I am strong. (2 Corinthians 12:8–10)

The prophet Jeremiah had learned this in a different way:

The word that came to Jeremiah from Yahweh as follows, "Get up and make your way down to the potter's house, and there I shall tell you what I have to say." So I went down to the potter's house; and there he was, working at the wheel. But the vessel he was making came out wrong, as may happen with clay when a potter is at work. So he began again and shaped it into another vessel, as he thought fit. Then the word of Yahweh came to me as follows, "House of Israel, can I not do to you what this potter does? Yahweh demands. Yes, like clay in the potter's hand, so you are in mine, House of Israel." (Jeremiah 18:1–6)

Biding God's time and getting on with life are ways of treating God as one who will not fail us. There is joy in living in anticipation of the ultimate outcome of everything, as the fourteenth-century English mystic, Julian of Norwich, knew:

And so our good Lord answered all the questions and doubts I could raise, saying most comfortingly: I may make all things well, and I can make all things well, and I shall make all things well, and I will make all things well; and you will see yourself that every manner of thing will be well. (*Showings*)

To trust God is to live more deeply. It frees us from wanting to know more than we need to know ahead of time:

Lead kindly Light,
    amid the encircling gloom…
The night is dark, and I am far from home…
I do not ask to see
    the distant scene;
    one step enough for me.
                    John Henry Newman

# For Practice

• Imagine the potter's hands, caressing, moulding, and redirecting you, the clay. Are there mistakes, hurts, or disappointments in your life that the Potter has reworked, or might want to rework? Whose "hands" do you expect the Potter might want to use?

• Find out more about Charles de Foucauld, and make his prayer (below) your own.

# For Prayer

Father, I abandon myself into your hands,
    do with me whatever you want.
For whatever you do,
    I thank you.
I am ready for, I accept, all.

Let only your will be done in me
    and in all your creatures,
    and I'll ask nothing else, my Lord.
Into your hands I commend my soul;
I give it to you, Lord, with the love of my heart,
    for I love you, my God,
    and so need to give,
    to surrender myself into your hands
    with a trust beyond all measure,
    because you are my Father.
                    Charles de Foucauld

# 21 The God Who Meets Us

We "come alive" to who we really are by knowing how much we mean to God. How much we mean to God is revealed above all in Jesus' life, from the manger in Bethlehem to his death on the cross. Our sense of who we really are and why we matter is linked to Christ.

Sometimes the Hebrew prophets used the image of a mother to emphasize God's closeness to us and care for us:

> Can a mother forget her infant, be without tenderness for the child of her womb? Yet even should she forget, still will I not forget you. (Isaiah 49:15)

> As nurslings, you shall be carried in her arms and fondled in her lap; As a mother comforts her son, so will I comfort you. (Isaiah 66:12–13)

But the real wonder of God's love, and therefore the wonder of ourselves, is in the fact that God's love was never owed to us. Sometimes it can seem to us as it did to Jesus, that God does not hear us. Aloud and in silent tears we pray to the One who has the power to make things different, but seems not to do so. We can mistakenly interpret this as God's "absence," when, in fact, it can be the experience of God's closeness. It is a moment of re-discovering that God, who has promised to be with us always, can only be close to us as the One whose presence is not owed to us, not "required" by us.

*The good experiences of life help us to enjoy the gift. But sometimes it is the painful experiences that remind us that life is a gift.*

What Moses discovered in his mystical experience of God's presence (Exodus 3) is central to the Jewish and Christian understanding of God, and it shows what the Jewish and Christian Scriptures mean by the name "Lord."

> Yahweh is not...a God whose function is to respond to our religious needs and satisfy our spiritual aspirations....Yahweh does not intervene in history or enter the human situation as if he were in any way required by history or by the situation. God comes down to us in our misery always as he came down to Moses in Midian, "to the westward part of the desert." He comes down with all the mystery that attaches to the concept of freedom when freedom is stretched to infinity....
>
> Precisely in the mysterious freedom of his presence Yahweh is manifested as the Lord, the one Lord of his own action, who does not abide man's questions because he stands beyond all questioning. In giving himself the name Yahweh, God forestalls the question that is somehow native to the heart of man, "why are you here?" or, in its more usual form, "why are you not here?" The answer, which refuses the question in both its forms, is: "I shall be there as who I am." (John Courtney Murray, *The Problem of God*)

Unlike the deities that natural religion tries to appease or win over to human agendas, and unlike the cosmic energy of New Age religion, the

God revealed in history is not there for our purposes or for our convenience—if and when it suits us. The journey into reality involves shedding all such illusions. The reality is a God whose love is all the more wonderful because it involves God's free choice.

This is also why prayer is not about trying to win God over or persuade God to look kindly on us. The kindness of God isn't really the problem:

> Since God did not spare his own Son but gave him up for the benefit of us all, we may be certain, after such a gift, that God will not refuse anything he can give. (Romans 8:32)

Friendship, on the other hand, takes two. Friends talk to each other. When we talk with God about our needs, we open ourselves to God's love, to wanting what God wants for us, and to moving further into the heart of the journey.

Experiencing the pain of God's seeming absence at times is part of coming closer to a God whose closeness cannot be demanded by us. Children who are taken to visit the poor, the lonely, the sick, and dying as well as taken to see the sunsets and the daffodils, will have a better start on the journey into reality than children who are shown only the delights. The good experiences of life help us to enjoy the gift. But sometimes it's the painful experiences that remind us that life *is* a gift.

# For Practice

• Ponder the mystery of God's extraordinary love, which is not owed to us in the first place, yet reaches into the depths and details of human history, reaching each of us personally, always forgiving.

# For Prayer

As a father has compassion on his children,
    so the Lord has compassion on the faithful.
For he knows of what we are made,
    remembers that we are dust.
Our days are like grass:
    like flowers of the field we blossom,
    the wind sweeps over us and we are gone,
    our place knows us no more.
But the Lord's kindness is forever.

*Psalm 103:13–17*

ALL OUR IDEAS OR CONCEPTS depend on our experience of created things, and so they are simply incapable of describing the One who is not a creature! God is always greater than human understanding. This is why the Scriptures use mainly images, likening God to a shepherd, a mother, a father, a potter, eagle's wings, a rock, a midwife, a lover, and many others.

Images nurture our faith better than ideas can. But they also need to be modified, broadened, and deepened as we pass from childhood faith to adult faith. Sometimes our disappointments come about because we have been depending too much on an image that was too limited. It is the image that has let us down, not God. So it is the image that needs to expand. It needs to be big enough to allow even for what happened on Good Friday.

# 22 Led By the Spirit

Jesus anticipated that you would need the Holy Spirit to enable you to recognize and properly interpret God's action in the world and in your life:

> The Advocate, the Holy Spirit, whom the Father will send in my name, will teach you everything and remind you of all I have said to you. (John 14:26)

It is also the Holy Spirit who enables us to recognize God's action in our own life:

> For the Spirit scrutinizes everything, even the depths of God. Among human beings, who knows what pertains to a person except the spirit of the person that is within? Similarly, no one knows what pertains to God except the Spirit of God. We have not received the spirit of the world but the Spirit that is from God, so that we may understand the things freely given us by God. (1 Corinthians 2:10–12)

For those who are led by the Spirit of God are children of God. For you did not receive a spirit of slavery to fall back into fear, but you received a spirit of adoption, through which we cry, "Abba, Father!" The Spirit itself bears witness with our spirit that we are children of God, and if children, then heirs, heirs of God and joint heirs with Christ, if only we suffer with him so that we may also be glorified with him....

In the same way, the Spirit too comes to the aid of our weakness; for we do not know how to pray as we ought, but the Spirit itself intercedes with inexpressible groanings. And the one who searches hearts knows what is the intention of the Spirit, because the Spirit intercedes for the holy ones according to God's will. (Romans 8:14–17, 26–27)

The steps we take on the journey into reality delicately combine personal responsibility and the work of God's Spirit working in us and in unison with us. This all takes place in the ordinary circumstances of our lives because our ordinary life, our mission in life, and our "spiritual" life are all made from the same material, the same events.

When we are unsure of the way, it helps to touch base with what we *are* sure of. Sometimes the confusion is only our lack of understanding, but at a deeper level we still have a sense for what is real. Then we must take responsibility for choosing reality. The more we are in touch with reality—reality of any kind— the more reality can touch and heal us.

Whatever leads to confusion, turmoil, or paralysis is not what God wants for you. Simply declining to go with such thoughts breaks their hold on you. Declining them is not the same as trying to push them away. Attempting to run away from our fears is the surest way of running right into them. To disempower our fears we first need to "own" them. In this way they lose their power to frighten us. Talking about them with a trusted friend can help this process. Sometimes it can help to stand outside our fear by speaking to it, or by looking at it and speaking to Jesus about it. The fear then gradually loses its hold.

> *Attempting to run away from our fears is the surest way of running right into them.*

Over time, it is possible to notice a pattern in your personal experience of God's dealings with you. In this pattern you discover and rediscover how God has been faithful to you. This discovery leads to deeper joy and gratitude. The challenge within it is to be faithful to what you see! You do this by trusting God in the times ahead of you. This is what it means to obey the Holy Spirit who has already accompanied you on a familiar and reliable path. This will take you to great heights. "Scaling the heights" is the kind of imagery mystics use to talk about the journey into reality, towards becoming the person God calls you to be—your true self:

> Believe steadfastly in what you have seen. Even if the way up to the High Places appears obscured and you are led to doubt whether you are following the right path, remember the promise: your ears shall hear a word behind you, saying, this is the way, walk in it, when you turn to the right and when you turn to the left. Always go forward along the path of obedience as far as you know it until I intervene, even if it seems to be leading you where you fear I could never mean you to go. (Hannah Hurnard, *Hinds' Feet on High Places*)

# For Practice

• In a journal, write down any events or times when God seemed to be especially present, or any insights into how God has been dealing with you, or any special grace you have received. Note, too, any fears or disappointments or crises that turned you towards God and what these led to. Continue to write in your journal as you see fit. After a few months, re-read what you have written in the context of prayer.

• Write a letter addressed to God about some event that has been significant for you, or write down what you think Jesus might be wanting to say to you.

# For Prayer

Lord, Holy Spirit,
   you blow like the wind
      in a thousand paddocks,
   inside and outside the fences,
   you blow where you wish to blow.

Lord, Holy Spirit,
   you are the sun who shines on the little plant,
   you warm him gently, you give him life,
   you raise him up to become a tree
      with many leaves.

Lord, Holy Spirit,
   you are the mother eagle with her young,
   holding them in peace under your feathers.
On the highest mountain
   you have built your nest,
      above the valley, above the storms of the world,
   where no hunter ever comes.

Lord, Holy Spirit,
   you are the bright cloud in whom we hide,
In whom we know already
   that the battle has been won.
You bring us to our brother Jesus
   to rest our heads upon his shoulder.

Lord, Holy Spirit,
You are the kind fire who does not cease to burn,
   consuming us with flames of love and peace,
Driving us out like sparks to set the world on fire.

Lord, Holy Spirit,
In the love of friends
   you are building a new house,
Heaven is with us when you are with us.
You are singing your song
   in the hearts of the poor.
Guide us, wound us, heal us.
Bring us to the Father.

James K. Baxter, *Song of the Holy Spirit*

# 23 Entering the Sufferings of Others

You are never more yourself than when you are "for others." It is part of your journey into reality. The joy Jesus experienced when he anticipated the outcome of his sufferings (see Hebrews 12:2) is the joy he shares with those who share his sufferings. It is not a coincidence that those who enter into the sorrows and sufferings of others discover a joy that is greater than mere happiness, i.e., the absence of suffering and sorrow.

Nor is it just coincidence that those who reach out to the most abandoned and most vulnerable members of society, or who spend years living with the poor in third-world conditions, are usually people who are themselves most alive to how much every person is loved by God.

"To suffer with" (sympathy or compassion) is to enter reverently into the feelings, hopes, and hurts of others until what happens to them feels as though it is happening to you, not in a way that is oppressive and unhealthy, but in a way that draws you further away from self-concern into the works of mercy, justice, and reconciliation.

Being a gift to others implies that we do not demand their acceptance of ourselves. If we are not freely accepted, we are not a gift. To demand acceptance would come from an unfulfilled need of our own.

So, too, wanting to give others assurances we can't honestly give comes from a need of our own and doesn't necessarily meet another's need. Sometimes we must admit that we don't have the answers. To accept that life is bigger than our understanding of it is to accept reality, and so enter more deeply into life. It is contact with life that is life-giving.

Giving without expecting anything in return becomes possible when we are secure in the knowledge that we are already fully loved. The key to all this is knowing how much you are loved by God:

> This is the love I mean: not our love for God, but God's love for us when he sent his Son. (1 John 4:10)

You did not have to earn God's love, and God loves you unconditionally. Knowing this is what frees you to love others without them having to deserve it, and love them unconditionally.

If you have not felt loved, there are good things in store for you. Let others love you. They are the embodiment (sacrament) of God's love for you.

In discovering that you are loved you feel more able to let yourself be known by trusted friends. Then you discover that you are still loved and respected in spite of what they know about you. Being more fully known and loved brings healing, growth, and freedom.

Look at yourself as Jesus sees you: let him tell you about the goodness he sees in you notwithstanding the defects. You begin to become what you feel and see in this experience.

*It is not a coincidence that those who enter into the sorrows and sufferings of others discover a joy that is greater than mere happiness....*

# For Practice

• There is another way of entering the sufferings of others. Next time you find yourself in conflict with someone, ask yourself what that person is feeling and perhaps, fearing. Then watch what happens to the conflict after you have put yourself in their shoes. This can make the experience of conflict enriching, and if forgiveness is involved, transforming.

• Who will be weeping, perhaps unknown to others, in your town tonight? Is there any way for you to show compassion to that person?

• Make your own the following verses from *The Servant Song* by Richard Gillard:

> Brother, sister, let me serve you
>   let me be as Christ to you.
> Pray that I might
>   have the grace to
>   let you be my servant too.
>
> We are pilgrims on a journey
> We're together on the road.
> We are here to help each other
>   walk the mile and bear the load.
>
> I will hold the Christ-light for you
>   in the night-time of your fear.
> I will hold my hand out to you
>   speak the peace you long to hear.
>
> I will weep when you are weeping
>   when you laugh I'll laugh with you.
> I will share your joy and sorrow
>   till we've seen this journey through.
>
> When we sing to God in heaven
>   we shall find such harmony
> born of all we've known together
> of Christ's love and agony.

# For Prayer

Let us see, O Lord, your mercy
  and give us your saving help.

I will hear what the Lord God has to say,
  a voice that speaks of peace,
  peace for his people and friends
  and those who turn to him in their hearts.

Mercy and faithfulness have met;
  justice and peace have embraced.
Faithfulness shall spring from the earth
  and justice look down from heaven.

*Psalm 85:7–11*

# 24 Let All Mortal Flesh Keep Silence

In the early chapters of this book you reflected on how everything looks different when you know how to see God in the world around you and in your own life. But this way of seeing needs to be practiced.

In a diffuse way, we can be aware of God's presence all the time. But we need occasionally to become aware of God's presence in a more focused way. Two people in love are continually aware of, and quietly enjoy, each other's company. Their love does not have to be intense all the time. But their presence to each other *does* need to be more focused, more direct, and more intense *some* of the time. Otherwise they slip into taking each other for granted.

We all have special moments in our relationship with God. Knowing we are in God's presence can affect us as it affected Moses when he felt the need to take off his shoes. He knew he was standing on "holy ground"—a metaphor for moments of greater awareness. At such times we have a sense of being personally loved because it is our own self that is in God's presence.

The point is not how you feel at such times. You might feel nothing! It is a matter of simply *knowing* that you are in God's presence—even if you feel nothing. When you are aware of being in God's presence, whatever happens next is prayer. It might be an expression of joy or thanksgiving or trust. It might be in words or song or silence.

*When you are aware of being in God's presence, whatever happens next is prayer.*

There is every chance you will feel lost for words. It doesn't matter: your whole being is responding to God's presence. You can, in the words of the Christian hymn, "Let all mortal flesh keep silence."

It works the other way as well: when you are surrounded by silence and stillness, you more easily become aware of God's presence. Creating such times is essential for the coming alive that results from "seeing" God.

> The frenetic activity of modern life with all its pressure makes it indispensable that Christians seek prayerful silence and contemplation, both as a condition for, and expression of, a vibrant faith. (Pope John Paul II, *Letter to the Church in Oceania*)

All sorts of things can prevent you from finding silence and stillness in your life. Advertisements constantly bombard your space and compete for your attention. The struggles and pressures of daily life can leave you with no time or energy for it. Anxiety, pain, and suffering can smother your efforts to think or to pray. People can be "dumbed down" by a constant diet of headlines, images, and sound-bites. It's like eating crackers all day instead of a balanced meal. In fact, it is worse, because it is one's deepest self that is being undernourished. It is even in the interests of some people to prevent others from taking the time to think beyond their immediate needs and experience. Consider, for example, the phrase "just do it," which implies "don't think."

Through the lack of opportunities for silence and stillness, we are deprived of opportunities to come alive to who we really are. There is more to our being than just doing, achieving, and having:

> In the course of their journey he came to a village, and a woman named Martha welcomed him into her house. She had a sister called Mary, who sat down at the Lord's feet and listened to him speaking. Now Martha, who was distracted with all the serving, came to him and said, "Lord, do you not care that my sister is leaving me to do the serving all by myself? Please tell her to help me." But the Lord answered, "Martha, Martha," he said, "you worry and fret about so many things, and yet few are needed, indeed only one. It is Mary who has chosen the better part, and it is not to be taken from her." (Luke 10:38–42)

The stillness we need can be found in many ways. Nature itself provides times and places that evoke wonder. The stillness inside an empty church can work powerfully upon us. Sometimes it is a matter of remembering, not in order to cling or to stay in the past, but to see God's fingerprints in our lives, even before we understood:

> Such are the feelings with which people often look back on their childhood, when some incident brings it vividly before them. Some relic or token of that early time, some spot, or some book, or a word, or a scent, or a sound, brings them back in memory to the first years of their discipleship, and then they see what they could not know at the time, that God's presence went with them and gave them rest. Even now perhaps they are unable to discern fully what it was which made that time so bright and glorious. They are full of tender, affectionate thoughts towards those first years, but they do not know why. They think it is those very years which they yearn after, whereas it is the presence of God which, as they now see, was then over them, which attracts them. (John Henry Newman, *Parochial and Plain Sermons*, vol. IV)

A Christian custom encourages us to spend a few moments of prayer at both ends of the day, upon rising in the morning and before going to bed at night. Kneeling down can make this prayer a more focused experience. Even if we don't know what to say, our body's posture acknowledges God.

At noon Christian tradition invites us to stand in awe of the incarnation, God's coming into our world in the person of Jesus Christ. This event is often recalled with the prayer known as the Angelus. We are amazed that God would come into our lives in this way, and amazed at how much we mean to God. We discover ourselves when we lose ourselves in this mystery.

# For Practice

• Try praying with your whole self, mind, body, and spirit. One way is to find a quiet place where you can lie flat on your face in God's presence. Let yourself be lost for words, and let your posture speak for you.

• In a quiet place, preferably a favorite spot, experience being the only person in the world and in the whole of human history, who is *you*.

# For Prayer

My soul is longing and yearning,
    is yearning for the courts of the Lord.
My heart and my soul ring out their joy
    to God, the living God.

The sparrow herself finds a home
    and the swallow a nest for her brood;
she lays her young by your altars.
They are happy who dwell in your house…
    as they go through the Bitter Valley
    they make it a place of springs.
                            *Psalm 84:2–4, 6*

# 25 A Deeper Solidarity

Is there any need greater—other than food, clothing, and shelter—than the need to belong? At the end of Chapter 14 we asked what chance there was of solidarity in a world bent on individual self-interest. To survive human tensions, solidarity needs to be rooted in a sharing of life that transcends human origins and has its source in God.

A sharing in Christ's life is the source of that solidarity that is needed for a civilization of love. After his resurrection, the disciples of Jesus continued to gather. They experienced what he meant when he promised to be with them whenever they came together. Coming into his life and coming into each other's lives were part of the same experience. The name we now use for this is "communion," which means a deep sharing of life with Christ and with one another. Christian life simply cannot be a private experience.

This communion extends to every aspect of our lives; what we do or fail to do for one another, we do or fail to do to Christ (Matthew 25:31–46). Knowing this affects the way we pray. It is hard to be at ease in God's presence if our relationships with others are wrong.

When we are with one another at prayer we experience solidarity in the same needs, fears, joys, and yearnings, and we find ourselves supported by one another's faith and hope and love. This can be an experience that is deeply moving, strong and convincing. It is an experience of solidarity with others that does not impinge on each other's privacy or freedom.

It is an experience that liberates us from the isolation of individualism, and makes us more willing and more able to be "for others." In turn, other people's acceptance of ourselves helps us to know that the meaning we believe our life has is not just an idea in our own head.

The community's rituals, teachings, and ministries draw us out of the isolation of private belief into the faith and spirituality of the Christian community. Above all, this communion is an experience of God's presence and of our coming alive because of it.

> The glory of God is human beings fully alive, and being fully alive is [comes from] seeing God. (Irenaeus)

Sometimes people might not have clear, articulate ideas about any of this. They just know it through being in touch with the reality itself, i.e., through their union with Christ and one another, especially in the community's worship—its liturgy.

Christian liturgy is not designed by the community for particular agendas or needs—not even the natural human need to worship. It is much more than gathering for prayers or sermons (even good ones) or fellowship. Liturgy connects us with events that took place in histo-

*It is not through self-centered introspection that we discover our real self. It is through the experience of being called and being sent that we discover who we really are.*

ry—the life, death, and resurrection of Christ. This is why its central prayers and symbols point to those events.

In the liturgy, our lives are connected to those events. The connection is real because the presence of Christ is real and the power of the Holy Spirit is real.

And so what began with the Father sending the Son and the Holy Spirit into the world now returns to the Father, through union with the Son and in the power of the Holy Spirit. We are drawn into what God is doing in human history and its wonderful outcome.

Through its liturgy the community itself is continually created, nurtured, and formed. We discover this personally through our "participation," letting ourselves become absorbed in what is taking place in the liturgy, taken up into it, given over to Christ present in it.

All this comes into focus especially in the celebration of Eucharist where we become "one body, one spirit in Christ" (Eucharistic Prayer III). This is our Christian identity. It is *belonging* at the deepest level of our selves. In the experience of solidarity—being for one another—we glimpse what it means to be human. This glimpse of what it means to be human helps us make the whole of life more human.

It is not through self-centered introspection that we discover our real self. It is through the experience of being called and being sent that we discover who we really are. And so the Christian community gathers (Chapter 26) in order to be dispersed (Chapter 27).

# For Practice

• Read John 15:1–17. What does this passage say to you about solidarity? What does it say about communion?

• Put aside, for the moment, all your images of the "Church." Now try to re-imagine the "Church" as an event: the gathering that happens around Jesus; who calls each of us to a personal relationship with him; that creates a new relationship with one another; in all our diversity; and draws us into the events of his life. The community which comes about in this way results from what Jesus and the Holy Spirit are doing in the world. (The English word "church" derives from the word the first Christians used to mean the "gathering" or "assembly." It was similar for the Jewish people; see Leviticus 23:4–7.)

# For Prayer

Sing to the Lord a new song,
    a hymn in the assembly of the faithful…
Let them praise his name in festive dance…
For the Lord takes delight in his people.
                                        *Psalm 149:1, 3, 4*

# 26 Gathered Around God's Word

At liturgy, the assembly gathers to hear God's word and respond to it. It is God's word that calls and forms the community that comes together. Christians believe that in the assembly it is still Christ who speaks when the Scriptures are proclaimed. It is a "live" word, not a mere recording of the past.

Christ's word is also embodied in those actions, called sacraments, in which Christ does what he says. For example, when Christ says (through those ordained or authorized to speak in his name), "your sins are forgiven," they are forgiven. When he says, in the celebration of Eucharist, "this is my body, this is my blood" (which is a way of emphasizing "it really *is* me"), then it really is.

Just as he did during his earthly life, the same Jesus, now risen, still reaches out, giving new life, renewed hope, forgiveness, healing, strength, and consolation. Sacraments make present, make visible, what he is saying and doing for us.

The reading of the Scriptures each Sunday builds up for the assembly a picture of how God has been present in the lives of other people. This makes it easier for us to recognize the signs of God's presence in our own lives. The homily that follows the readings is different from a sermon. Sermons tell people what *they* should be doing; a homily points to what *God* is doing in our own lives. Seeing the signs of God's presence in our own lives makes us want to praise, thank, and trust God.

*We come to faith more fully in the community of faith.*

In the liturgy, the Scriptures become a kind of mirror where we see ourselves in the light of God's purposes. The Church holds this mirror up at different angles during the various seasons and feasts of the Christian year, always reflecting the way God is present in people's lives, including our own. To walk away from the mirror where we are revealed to ourselves is to walk out on ourselves.

Part of our response to God's word is our profession of faith. By declaring what we believe we declare who we are. Christians are not the only ones included in God's wonderful plan. But they have the privilege of knowing the plan God has revealed in the life, death, and resurrection of Jesus. This is a privilege they want to share with others.

The practices of the faith form an environment of faith. In that environment we are able to experience the certainty of faith. This certainty cannot be known from the outside looking in. We come to faith more fully in the community of faith. Its faith, which had its origins in the life, death, and resurrection of Jesus, becomes our faith.

The community's understanding of the gospel gradually becomes our own understanding. Participation in the life of the Church and the formation of a Christian conscience take place together. The community also grows in its understanding of the faith. It can be sure of its faith even before it fully understands.

# For Practice

- Reflect on how you would expect a Christian's conscience to be different even though God's law is the same for all.

# For Prayer

*Reflect on this passage, and make these words your own.*

Blessed be the God and Father of our Lord Jesus Christ, who has blessed us in Christ with every spiritual blessing in the heavens, as he chose us in him, before the foundation of the world, to be holy and without blemish before him. In love he destined us for adoption to himself through Jesus Christ, in accord with the favor of his will, for the praise of the glory of his grace that he granted us in the beloved. In him we have redemption by his blood, the forgiveness of sins, in accord with the riches of his grace that he lavished upon us. In all wisdom and insight, he has made known to us the mystery of his will in accord with his favor that he set forth in him as a plan for the fullness of times, to sum up all things in Christ, in heaven and on earth.                    *Ephesians 1:3–10*

CHRISTIANS LIVE BY TWO CALENDARS: one that marks the days, weeks, and seasons according to the movement of the earth around the sun; and another that commemorates the events that give meaning to all this. Our awareness of salvation history becomes part of our journey through time.

- During the season of Advent, Christians "re-live" the period during which the Jewish people waited and prepared themselves for the coming of the promised Savior. The Scripture readings and prayers of the Advent season deepen our own longing for his coming. In this way we open our lives to him, "until he comes again."

- At Christmas we re-live with wonder the fact that God has personally entered our history and done so in this intimately human way.

- During Lent we prepare ourselves by prayer, fasting, and generosity for the holy season of Easter. Receiving the gifts of God involves being open to them, and being sorry for the times we have closed ourselves off from God.

- In Holy Week we accompany Jesus through the last days of his earthly life, including his last supper with his disciples, followed by his prayer in the garden, then his arrest and crucifixion.

- The highlight of the Christian calendar is Easter when we celebrate the resurrection of Jesus and our own future resurrection, for he was "the first fruits of many brothers and sisters" (1 Corinthians 15:20–23).

- By celebrating his ascension, we celebrate his "return to the Father" taking our human nature with him, and his "going on ahead of us to prepare a place for us" (John 14:1–3).

- Pentecost celebrates the coming of the Holy Spirit who gathers us into the unity of Christ's body. In union with Christ we have "confident access to the Father" (Ephesians 3:12).

# 27 Sent Out

To find yourself you are going to have to lose yourself. The community that gathers to be nurtured by word and sacrament is then sent out. Union with Christ is to be lived. Through your union with Christ the whole of your life is being drawn into your relationship with God. Every aspect of it becomes an offering worthy of God. Unless it comes to this, we are worshiping God only with our lips.

At the supper Jesus had with his apostles on the night before he died, he told them he was about to give his life for them:

> This is my body given up for you…my blood poured out for many…Do this in memory of me. (Luke 22:19–20)

In this way, his love would become present in the lives of his followers. Augustine put it nicely: "when we receive the body and blood of Christ we become what we receive." We become the body "given up for others." We become the blood or life "poured out for others." Our "holy communion" involves this commitment. You are your true self—a gift to others—most of all when you are the body of Christ, when his self-giving is embodied in your self-giving.

In your life, his mission is made present today:

> He came to Nazara, where he had been brought up, and went into the synagogue on the Sabbath day as he usually did. He stood up to read, and they handed him the scroll of the prophet Isaiah. Unrolling the scroll he found the place where it is written:
>
> "The spirit of the Lord is on me,
>   for he has anointed me
>   to bring the good news to the afflicted.
> He has sent me to bring good news to the poor,
>   to proclaim liberty to captives
>   and to the blind new sight,
>   to set the down-trodden free,
>   to proclaim the Lord's year of favor…."
> Then he began to speak to them, "this text is being fulfilled today even while you are listening." (Luke 4:16–21)

This text is being fulfilled today whenever the lame (including those crippled by fear, anxiety, or loneliness), the captives (including those held captive by obsessions and addictions), and the blind (including those who live in the dark of not being sure whether their lives are worthwhile), hear the good news of God's love for them made present in *your* love for them.

*God's love for the world takes the form of your love to transform it.*

According to Mother Teresa, the greatest poverty and suffering isn't not belonging; it is having no one who cares. Only love can change this. Because you are the body of Christ, it is Christ who touches other people's lives through your compassion and forgiveness and the hope you bring them. In fact, his grace and reconciliation can only flow into your life if they flow through your life into the lives of others.

> It is all God's work. It was God who reconciled us to himself through Christ and gave us the

work of handing on this reconciliation. In other words, God in Christ was reconciling the world to himself, not holding people's faults against them, and he has entrusted to us the news that they are reconciled. So we are ambassadors for Christ; It is as though God were appealing through us, and the appeal we make in Christ's name is: be reconciled to God. (2 Corinthians 5:18–20)

Since your very being is a gift, you are never more true to your self than when *you* are a gift, freely and lovingly there for others. This is the very opposite of imposing on others, possessing them, dominating or using them. It is a way of being that opens up into a "civilization of love." God's love for the world takes the form of your love to transform it.

> Evangelization would not be complete if it did not take account of the unceasing interplay of the gospel and of our concrete lives, both personal and social. That is why evangelization involves an explicit message...about the rights and duties of every human being, about family life...about life in society, about international life, peace, justice, and development... and liberation. (Pope Paul VI, *Letter on Evangelization*)

Our deeds of justice, mercy, and reconciliation become the signs, or language, that speak to people about what they were really made for, namely the fullness of love and life, truth, freedom, and peace. That fullness is not possible as long as our death is still in front of us. In the meantime, our deeds are the language that tells.

# For Practice

• Jot down some notes on any connections you see among being called, being sent, and being your true self.

• Read Celia Lashlie's book *The Journey to Prison: Who Goes and Why*, and as you read it try to identify the poor, the captives, the blind, and the downtrodden in your town or neighborhood.

# For Prayer

Lord,
Open our eyes to the needs of all;
    inspire us with words and deeds
    to comfort those who labor
      and are burdened;
    keep our service of others
    faithful to the example of Christ.
Let your Church be a living witness
    to truth and freedom, to justice and peace,
    that all people may be lifted up
    by the hope of a world made new.
*From a Eucharistic Prayer of the Catholic Mass*

# 28 Catholic

How Christian is Christian? The core of all Christian life, and the life of all Christians, is the *presence* of the risen Christ drawing us into his own life. Being Catholic does not add to being Christian, but it takes very seriously all the ways God chooses to be present to us.

As a hedge against idolatry, some Christians have been cautious about associating God too closely with created things. But whenever Christians have disdained any aspect of creation or of human nature, the Catholic Church has reaffirmed the goodness of everything God has made.

> The Catholic sacramental vision "sees" God in all things—other people, communities, movements, events, places, objects, the environment, the world at large, the historical…. Indeed, for Catholicism it is only in and through these material realities that we can encounter the invisible God. (Richard McBrien, *Catholicism*)

Moreover, God's presence is always "for us and for our salvation" (Nicene Creed); it graces our existence. As a hedge against any semblance of magic, some Christians prefer to think of God's saving action as directly touching our inner "spiritual" selves. But in the Catholic tradition, God's actions grace whatever they touch. The human body, sexuality, art, music, dance, and celebration, as well as sickness and suffering, can be symbols through which God touches our lives.

Christianity is not a spirituality apart from the human body or above the human condition or independent of the Christian community. "The Word was made flesh…": thus, the God whose presence is never owed to us has nevertheless chosen to be very close to us. The incarnation is about God reaching into the depths of our human situation.

The community Christ still gathers around him includes sinners and saints; it is not a spiritual elite. This is the body of Christ in which Christ is present. Perhaps it's not surprising, therefore, that Christ appoints people to act in his name who are ordinary and weak:

> …for it is not ourselves that we are preaching, but Christ Jesus as the Lord, and ourselves as your servants for Jesus' sake….We are only the earthenware jars that hold this treasure, to make clear that such an overwhelming power comes from God and not from us. (2 Corinthians 4:5, 7)

Notwithstanding their weaknesses, Jesus appointed his apostles to speak in his name: welcoming them would be welcoming him (see Luke 10:16). The faith entrusted to the apostles is made present in the life of the faith community. Even those who teach the faith must first learn it from the community.

The Catholic tradition understands that the apostles' role as pastors and teachers is now made present in the role of the bishops when they teach the same faith, using the words of different times and cultures, and apply that teaching to new cir-

---

*Being Catholic does not add to being Christian, but it takes very seriously all the ways God chooses to be present.*

cumstances. The role of "confirming the brethren" given to Peter (Luke 22:32) is now made present in the role of the bishop of Rome. (Peter himself was already dead by the time his role was recorded in the gospels of Matthew and Luke.)

In the Catholic tradition, ordination is not mere delegation by the community to act in its name; the Holy Spirit confers the role of making visible *what Christ is doing* in and for the community. Like Christ, those whose ministry is to make his role visible are to be the servants and the least of all (Mark 10:42–45). At the last supper when commissioning his disciples to "do this in memory of me," he symbolized his and their servant role by washing their feet. Lording it over others, which had been the hallmark of sin from the beginning, ("he shall rule over you," Genesis 3:16) was being replaced by "he shall serve you."

To honor the fact that Christ's sacrifice on the cross was sufficient for our salvation (and does not need to be added to or repeated in any way), some Christians have been wary about calling the celebration of Eucharist a "sacrifice." But for Catholics, it is Christ's offering of himself on the cross made present. The sacramental signs of this presence are the ritual meal we celebrate in remembrance of him.

> Because he remains forever, (Jesus) has a priesthood that does not pass away. He is always able to save those who approach God through him, since he lives forever to make intercession for them. (Hebrews 7:24–25)

When Catholics gather, it is not just for prayer or preaching or fellowship. It is because the liturgy connects our lives with the events of Christ's life, death, and resurrection through his presence.

The real presence of Christ is highlighted in the Catholic practice of reserving the holy Eucharist outside of Mass for people's devotion, and making this available to people through perpetual adoration. In this way, the real presence of Christ is very focused. Knowing that he is really here, knowing that he is the same Jesus who was present to his first disciples, and knowing that he is the Son of God has a powerful impact on the pray-er, leading to deeper prayer and adoration.

# For Practice

• If there is one near you, spend some time before Christ in a chapel of perpetual adoration. Know that he is really there for you, that this is the same Jesus we know through Scripture, and that he is the Son of God.

• Read the letter to the Hebrews in the New Testament. Reflect on its meaning in your life today.

# For Prayer

Come, let us joyfully sing to the Lord;
   cry out to the rock of our salvation.
Let us greet him with a song of praise,
   joyfully sing out our psalms.

Come, then, let us bow down and worship,
   bending the knee before the Lord, our maker.
For this is our God, and we are his people,
   the flock that God shepherds.

*Psalm 95:1–2, 6–7*

# 29 Can Sinners Belong?

When Jesus invited Simon Peter to be one of his closest companions, Peter objected because he felt unworthy: "depart from me, Lord, I am a sinful man" (Luke 5:8). But Jesus wanted Peter just the same. And that was only the start: the criticism most often leveled against Jesus by the religious leaders of the day was that he "mixed with sinners."

Years later, Matthew's gospel made a special feature of Jesus' ancestry, opening with a majestic announcement: "the story of the origin of Jesus Christ, son of David, son of Abraham…." Then it goes on to link Jesus with an unlikely lot, including liars and cheats, betrayers and prostitutes.

> As for gloriously reigning monarchs of the house of David, of the fourteen Judean kings that Matthew lists between David and deportation, only two…could be considered as faithful to God's standards.…The rest were an odd assortment of idolaters, murderers, incompetents, power-seekers, and harem-wastrels. David himself was a stunning combination of saint and sinner. There was, of course, the arranged murder of Bathsheba's husband so that David might possess the wife legally. Even more indicative of David's shrewd piety was his personal innocence combined with mafia-like politics whereby his relatives murdered opponents for him.…
>
> This curious story of a Davidic monarchical institution that had divine origins but was frequently corrupt, venal, and uninspiring, was also part of "the story of the origin of Jesus Christ." (Raymond Brown, "The Genealogy of Jesus Christ," in *Worship*, November 1986)

*There is only one thing worse than allowing sinners to know they belong; it is making them feel they don't belong.*

The gospel writer could have politely skipped over some of these characters. More worthy people could have been included. But the gospel is simply comfortable with the fact that human sinfulness is not what ultimately counts. What counts is what God is doing—writing straight with our crooked lines. Human sinfulness is overturned by God's mercy and forgiveness.

Raymond Brown further notes that in Jesus' genealogy, coming closer to his own time, we find

> a collection of unknown people whose names never made it into sacred history for having done something significant. In other words, while powerful rulers in the monarchy brought God's people to a low point in recorded history (the deportation), unknown people, presumably also proportionately divided among saints and sinners, were the ones through whom God brought restoration. This is yet another indicator of the unpredictability of God's grace that accomplishes God's purposes through those whom others regard as unimportant and forgettable.

That is how it was leading up to Jesus. And that is how it has been ever since. Sometimes people have been "scandalized" because it seemed so easy for sinners to feel at home in the Catholic Church. In spite of feeling unworthy or unholy, they have known they still belong.

Sin and failure, followed by repentance and reform, and then more sin and failure, have been the story of the Church. This goes back even to the beginning if we include Judas and Peter and

Levi and Mary Magdalene. So it would be a sad day if people who are struggling with sin of one kind or another felt the Church was meant only for respectable people, and that they themselves didn't qualify. There is only one thing worse than allowing sinners to know they belong; it is making them feel they *don't* belong.

It is not as if sin doesn't matter, or that living a good life doesn't matter. The point is *why* they matter. In Jesus' time, the religious leaders thought that through their good works and good lives they earned God's favor. But it's the other way around. A good life is what we want to live when we discover that we don't have to earn God's favor, because it is all gift. Good works are the works of faith because they come from knowing God loves us.

> God, being rich in faithful love, through the great love with which he loved us, even when we were dead in our sins, brought us to life with Christ—it is through grace that you have been saved—and raised us up with him and gave us a place with him in heaven, in Christ Jesus. This was to show for all ages to come through his goodness towards us in Christ Jesus, how extraordinarily rich he is in grace. Because it is by grace that you have been saved, through faith; not by anything of our own, but by a gift from God; not by anything that you have done, so that nobody can claim the credit. We are God's work of art, created in Christ Jesus for the good works which God has already designated to make up our way of life. (Ephesians 2:4–10)

Not to live that kind of life is to exclude one's self from what God is doing in the world.

Jesus' rejection of sin and his acceptance of sinners live on in what Catholics call the sacrament of penance, or reconciliation. This sacrament brings us to the point of confessing our sins and being sorry for them, which includes a willingness to do better and to repair any harm we have done by our sins. When you name an unpleasant truth about yourself and then find that instead of being thought less of you are received with understanding, respect, and forgiveness, you experience what others experienced when they heard Jesus say to them: "Go in peace, your sins are forgiven."

In this sacrament, it is still Jesus who says this, through one who has been ordained to make present what he is doing. Knowing this is deeply reassuring, and is a reason for joy and thanksgiving. It is also empowering for the journey still in front of you:

> I will sprinkle clean water upon you to cleanse you from all your impurities, and from all your idols I will cleanse you. I will give you a new heart and place a new spirit within you, taking from your bodies your stony hearts and giving you natural hearts. I will put my spirit within you and make you live by my statutes, careful to observe my decrees. (Ezekiel 36:25–27)

# For Practice

• Read Jesus' daring description of God's desire to forgive in Luke 15:11–32, the story of the prodigal son. Reflect on a time when you were touched by the forgiveness of another.

# For Prayer

I thank you, God, with all my heart,
    you have heard the words of my mouth.
In the presence of your angels I will bless you;
    I will adore before your holy temple.

I thank you for your faithfulness and love
    which are greater than all we ever knew of you.
On the day I called, you answered;
    you increased the strength of my soul.
*Psalm 138:1–3*

# 30 Particular Callings

The question, "Who are you really?" is connected to the purpose God had in mind when calling you into existence. You are the person God wanted for that purpose. And so, discovering God's purpose is the same as discovering who you really are. We saw earlier that God's hopes for you and your own deepest desires are actually the same, and we saw how God makes these known to you (see chapter 17). Now let's look at how this works.

People who are good at a sport or music or a craft often say it is something they love doing. The sacrifices they make and the hours they put into training are possible because they love what they are doing. Love makes a difference. It is the same for following one's vocation, i.e., fulfilling the purpose of one's life. Love is what makes it possible. People who realize how wonderful the gift of life is, and how wonderful the Giver is, can find themselves in love with God and all that God has made. It is love that accounts for the sacrifices they are willing to make. And who is going to put a limit on love?

God's love has gone well beyond what was owing or necessary or "reasonable." Those who see this can find themselves going beyond normal limits. After all, people in love do crazy things! Love can't be reduced to something measured, calculated, or self-interested.

The special vocation of Christian husbands and wives is to mirror Christ's own love for all of us. On the cross, God's love is revealed as self-giving, unconditional, forgiving, faithful to the end, and life-giving. By their marriage vows, Christian husbands and wives commit themselves to that kind of love, to being a sign of what God's love is like (see Ephesians 5:28–33).

Every Christian vocation participates in Christ's own mission; it is a way of "being for others."

> The Holy Spirit writes in the heart and in the life of every baptized person a project of love and grace, which is the only way to give full meaning to our existence. (Pope John Paul II)

*Discovering God's purpose is the same as discovering who you really are.*

Some choose a dedicated single life as a way of being "for others." By giving up perfectly good options, including marriage, they make a statement with their lives: that even the good things of life don't fully satisfy the human heart; we are made for more.

Many take vows and become religious sisters or brothers, supporting each other in community. They opt for a form of poverty and powerlessness that can move mountains.

There are people with power and wealth who can, at the stroke of a pen, eliminate jobs and make other people "superfluous." Then there are people like the late Mother Teresa of Calcutta. Empty-handed, she brought vision and hope to places where there seemed to be only hopelessness and death. And the world respected her for this. When the history books of the future are written, her name will be remembered, while the people at the top of industry and commerce probably won't even make the footnotes. It's not that she was "different" from you and I. She started her life the same way we did. She was a very ordinary person, with even fewer opportunities than most of us have had.

Historically, religious sisters and brothers have been at the frontiers of providing education, hospitals, orphanages, and other forms of social ministry. Throughout the years, many other wonderful people, including other Christians and people of other faiths, have done similar things, but often as individuals. But religious communities have been able to continue these works beyond the lifetime of individuals. Today, governments and other organizations have taken over many of these works, and so communities of religious sisters and brothers look for new ways of ministering to human needs. Only the shapes and forms of religious life are changing.

History shows that whenever Christians have lost their enthusiasm or become lax, movements of renewal and reform have sprung up. These have taken many different forms, but all have involved a return to the stark challenges of the gospel. Some of today's new movements involve loose-knit forms of community between individuals, married couples, families, and celibates who have consecrated themselves to living by the gospel while remaining at homes and at work. These "movements" are ways of experiencing communion more deeply. This helps the whole Christian community to recognize its own vocation to share Christ's life.

Another way of being for others is to become a priest. To describe his own role in our lives, Jesus pictured himself as the good shepherd. In his time, the shepherd led his small flock out at the beginning of each day. Then he spent the whole day with them, leading them to better pastures. It was a very intimate relationship. He knew each sheep by name and they knew him. They knew he would help them, and they trusted him. He was there for them.

This is the image that the Church has used ever since to picture the role of those it calls "pastors." Sometimes, priests have fallen short of this ideal. (And sometimes they receive more publicity than all the others who have faithfully given their lives for their people.)

To underline the importance of practicing what they preach priests are asked to put their lives where their mouths are. That is what celibacy is about. It is a way of saying "what I want you to know about God's love for you is so wonderful that I am prepared to stake everything for it."

A vocation to priesthood is not about being a special person; everyone is special. Nor is it about being "worthy"; indeed, no one is. It *is* about making visible what Jesus still does for his people. It, too, is a commitment, not just something one does because he "feels like it." The pleasure comes later on, at those moments when you rejoice deeply because you have done something very special for someone, something that will matter to them forever and for which they came to you because you were a priest.

Someone who thinks they might be called to the priesthood does not need to know straight away if they are suitable, because others will help them decide that. After all, a vocation is not just about what we want to do. It is a calling from God through the Church.

The only question each person must be able to answer (one that no one else can answer for us or her) is "Am I willing?" Christ does the rest, no matter now ordinary we are. He's got a way of revealing his power through human weakness (see 2 Corinthians 12:9–10).

# For Practice

- Slowly and thoughtfully read the following Scripture passage. Then, in prayer, speak with Jesus about what he meant when he said these things (let him do some of the talking):

*After this the Lord appointed seventy-two others and sent them out ahead of him in pairs, to all the towns and places he himself would be visiting. And he said to them, "The harvest is rich but the laborers are few, so ask the Lord of the harvest to send laborers to do his harvesting. Start off now, but look, I am sending you out like lambs among* wolves. *Take no purse with you, no haversack, no sandals. Salute no one on the road. Whatever house you enter, let your first words be, 'Peace to this house!' And if a man of peace lives there, your peace will go and rest on him; if not, it will come back to you. Stay in the same house, taking what food and drink they have to offer, for the laborer deserves his wages; do not move from house to house. Whenever you go into a town where they make you welcome, eat what is put before you. Cure those in it who are sick, and say, 'The kingdom of God is very near to you.'*

*The seventy-two came back rejoicing. "Lord," they said, "even the devils submit to us when we use your name." He said to them, "I watched Satan fall like lightning from heaven. Look, I have given you power to tread down serpents and scorpions and the whole strength of the enemy; nothing shall ever hurt you. Yet do not rejoice that the spirits submit to you; rejoice instead that your names are written in heaven."*

*Just at this time, filled with joy by the Holy Spirit, he said, "I bless you, Father, Lord of heaven and of earth, for hiding these things from the learned and the clever and revealing them to little children. Yes, Father, for that is what it has pleased you to do. Everything has been entrusted to me by my Father; and no one knows who the Son is except the Father, and who the Father is except the Son and those to whom the Son chooses to reveal him."*

*Then turning to his disciples he spoke to them by themselves, "Blessed are the eyes that see what you see, for I tell you that many prophets and kings wanted to see what you see, and never saw it; to hear what you hear, and never heard it."* (Luke 10:1–9, 17–24)

• Contemplate the scene painted by Matthew 14:22–33, where the disciples were in the boat being tossed about by the waves. During the fourth watch of the night Jesus came toward them. When they saw him walking on the water they were terrified. His reassuring words to them lifted Peter to another level. He heard Jesus say to them: "Be of good heart, it is I; don't be afraid." Faith in Jesus' word enabled Peter to forget all else. He forgot the dangers, he forgot what others might say, he forgot himself and replied, "Lord, if it is you let me come to you upon the waters." And Jesus said, "Come."

# For Prayer

"What can bring us happiness?" many say.
Let the light of your face shine on us, O Lord.
You have put into my heart a greater joy
   than they have from abundance
   of corn and new wine.
I will lie down in peace and sleep comes at once
   for you alone, Lord, make me dwell in safety.
Psalm 4:6–8

**The Galilee Song**
As I gaze into the night,
   down the future of my years,
I'm not sure I want to walk
   past horizons that I know!
But I feel my spirit called
   like a stirring deep within,
Restless 'til I live again
   beyond the fears that close me in!

*Refrain*
So I leave my boats behind!
Leave them on familiar shores!
Set my heart upon the deep!
Follow you again, my Lord!

Frank Andersen

# Appendix
## Interpreting the Bible

You might wish to reflect further on who you really are by using the Bible. But, as you know, confusion and harm can come about from misinterpreting the Scriptures. A few basic facts can help you to avoid misunderstanding. For Christians, the Bible is the word of God. God's word comes to us in human words. So we need to understand the human meaning to properly hear what God wants us to know.

To understand the human meaning, we need to recognize that the Bible contains many different ways of speaking. In fact, it is more like a library than a single book. It contains different kinds of literature: historical narrative, fiction, poetry, biography, drama, and so on. To treat them all the same is to misuse the Bible. This happens when every sentence is regarded as a divine message or a divine instruction without regard for the different kinds of literature contained therein.

The human meaning depends on what the original authors meant and how they thought. For example, when people experience some event, there is both the external event itself—what happened—and the inward experience of how it affected them. A modern novelist can describe the psychology of the inner experience. But ancient authors could not do that. So in order to do justice to what the event meant to them, they sometimes exaggerated the external details. Dramatization and hyperbole sometimes communicate the meaning of an event better than mere documentation does.

What makes these different writings one book is their origin in the faith of a people—a people who believed God was involved in their history.

Their Scriptures were an expression of their faith, part of their tradition.

The writings of the New Testament are expressions of the faith of the Christian communities, dating back to the lifetime of the apostles or to people who had known the apostles. The Scriptures do not exist separately from the faith community; they are inspired accounts of the faith of the Christian communities. Still, today, the faith of the Christian community worldwide is the touchstone for knowing the true interpretation of the Scriptures. Sometimes the Scriptures on their own are open to more than one interpretation.

The four gospels are a unique kind of literature. They are based on the things that Jesus said and did, but they are not pure biographies. Most of the text is a careful adaptation of what Jesus said and did, made after his disciples had come to understand them. Their understanding was affected dramatically by their experience of his resurrection. That put a new light on everything they had experienced during his lifetime.

Adaptation also resulted from the way the Christian communities used Jesus' teachings when they preached to others or instructed them. The different endings given to some of Jesus' parables reflect their practice of adapting his teachings to different situations (see Matthew 22:1–14, and Luke 14:15–24). Further "adaptation" occurred when the individual writers of the gospels selected from the oral tradition what they wanted to include in their written gospel. Their selection depended on whom they were writing for (for example, Jews who already knew the Hebrew Scriptures, or Gentiles, who didn't).

Sometimes, what they included or left out depended on their central theme and main reason for writing. Matthew, Mark, Luke, and John each had their own purpose.

Both the ancient Hebrew authors and the early Christian authors were writing about what had been revealed through God's involvement in human history. God's purposes were revealed in the things God did. The Scriptures are like a cover letter that accompanies and interprets God's actions. What God does is always greater than what words can say.

Human words and concepts are drawn from human experience, and so what lies beyond human experience is difficult to talk about. That is why the writers of the Bible often used stories to evoke a sense of what they were pointing to. In this sense, the story symbolizes the teaching.

Some biblical stories are purely fictional; they were composed to teach an important truth. But the truth they teach doesn't depend on the story being historical. Jesus' parables are like that. So, too, is the story of Jonah. There are other biblical stories that were written precisely because an extraordinary thing *did happen*. Because the event was outside ordinary human experience, they needed to build a story around it. The accounts of Jesus' resurrection and of his appearances after the resurrection, as well as the accounts of his virginal conception are stories of this kind.

Both kinds of story—the kind that is purely fictional (like the parables) and the kind that is based on something that actually happened (like Jesus' resurrection) point beyond themselves to what the authors wanted us to know. The details of the story are not the point. For example, the creation stories teach that God is our creator, with all the consequences of that. The authors are not teaching us *how* God created, even though the story could give that impression.

Finally, while it is necessary to understand the human meaning to understand God's word, it is even more necessary to approach the word of God with faith:

No one knows what pertains to God except the Spirit of God. We have not received the spirit of the world but the Spirit that is from God, so that we may understand the things freely given us by God. (1 Corinthians 2:11–12)

# For Practice

• Read and enjoy the book of Job. In what ways can you relate to his life, his feelings, and his actions?

# For Prayer

Attend, my people, to my teaching;
 listen to the words of my mouth.
I will open my mouth in story,
 drawing lessons from of old.
We have heard them, we know them;
 our ancestors have recited them to us.
We do not keep them from our children;
 we recite them to the next generation,
 the praiseworthy and mighty deeds
  of the Lord,
 the wonders that he performed....
That they too might put their trust in God.

*Psalm 78:1–4, 7*